101 QUESTIONS

ABOUT SEX AND SEXUALITY... WITH ANSWERS FOR THE CURIOUS, CAUTIOUS, AND CONFUSED

101

QUESTIONS ABOUT

SEX

AND SEXUALITY . . .
WITH ANSWERS FOR THE CURIOUS,
CAUTIOUS, AND CONFUSED

. . . . .

FAITH HICKMAN BRYNIE

. . . . . .

TWENTY-FIRST CENTURY BOOKS

BROOKFIELD, CONNECTICUT

Published by Twenty-First Century Books
A Division of The Millbrook Press, Inc.
2 Old New Milford Road
Brookfield, CT   06804
www.millbrookpress.com

Cover photograph courtesy of © Sharon Swanson
Photographs courtesy of Phototake: p. 14 (© Gopal Murti); Department of Anatomy,
University of Bristol: p. 16; © 2002 A.D.A.M., Inc.: p. 50; Photo Researchers, Inc.: pp. 52
(© Biophoto Associates), 133 (© Eye of Science); Corbis: pp. 54 (© AFP), 94 (top © Michel
Arnaud; bottom © Mitchell Gerber); Media Photo Group, Inc.: p. 59; Dr. Judith Langlois:
p. 61; Pat Barclay: p. 62; Christopher P. Goscin, B.S., College of Medicine at the University
of South Florida; Claudia G. Berman, M.D., Robert A. Clark, M.D., Radiology Service at
the H. Lee Moffitt Cancer Center & Research Institute, Tampa, FL: p. 75; Curran J. Smith,
M.D., Seattle, WA, YourNaturalBeauty.com: p. 76; Visuals Unlimited, Inc.: p. 80 (© Fred E.
Hossler); The University of Texas Medical Branch at Galveston: p. 89 (Photograph by John
Glowczwski); Retna Ltd. USA: p. 93 (left © Gary Lewis/Camera Press; right © Jeff
Slocomb); From "The Neural Basis of Romantic Love" by A. Bartels and S. Zeki, published
in *NeuroReport* 11(17): 3829-3834: p. 98; © Jeannette May: p. 108 (produced by Jeannette
May with Coalition for Positive Sexuality); PhotoEdit: p. 117 (© Michael Newman); ©
2001 Men Can Stop Rape: p. 122 (Poster image from the Strength Campaign produced in
Washington, D.C., by Men Can Stop Rape. Photograph by Jim Varriale); The National
Campaign to Prevent Teen Pregnancy and *Teen People* magazine: p. 140. Diagrams by
Sharon Lane Holm.

Library of Congress Cataloging-in-Publication Data
Brynie, Faith Hickman, 1946–
101 questions about sex and sexuality— : with answers for the curious, cautious, and
 confused / by Faith Hickman Brynie.
p. cm.
Summary: Uses a question-and-answer format to present information about the physical,
emotional, and social topics surrounding sex and sexuality.
Includes bibliographical references and index.
ISBN 0-7613-2310-4
1. Sex instruction for youth. 2. Youth—Sexual behavior. 3. Sex. [1. Sex. 2. Sex instruction
for youth. 3. Questions and answers.] I. Title: One hundred one questions about sex and
sexuality. II. Title: One hundred and one questions about sex and sexuality. III. Title.
HQ35 .B8223 2003   306.7—dc21   2002011209

CONTENTS

ACKNOWLEDGMENTS

Wrote Lewis Gizzard in his classic *Don't Bend Over in the Garden, Granny, You Know Them Taters Got Eyes* (Villard Books, 1989): "Even I'm smart enough to know you don't go dedicating a book about sex to anybody." Gizzard's point is well taken, so a formal dedication is missing from this book. Gratitude, however, is not. The author appreciates the kind and unselfish contributions of all those who helped.

Thanks to Jill Losee-Hoehlein, Great Bridge High School, Chesapeake, Virginia, and her school's family-living students for the questions they provided. Thanks, also, to all those young people who provided questions anonymously via the Internet. There would be no book without them.

On matters of law, the author is grateful for guidance provided by Dr. Paul H. Robinson, professor of law, Northwestern University, Chicago. Jennifer Barefoot of the Kaiser Family Foundation provided invaluable help with legal research. Thanks to Dr. Robert Brooks, evolutionary biologist, University of New South Wales in Australia, and to Pat Barclay, McMaster University, Hamilton, Ontario, Canada, for sharing their research data and results. Appreciation to Erika Lambert, family physician in Harrisburg, North Carolina, for sending her survey of students' knowledge of the human papillomavirus and to Professor Andreas Bartels, Wellcome Department of Cognitive Neurology, University College, London, for his MRI pictures of brains in love. Special thanks to Deborah Roffman, sexuality education teacher in Baltimore, Maryland, and author of *Sex and Sensibility*, for her wisdom on matters of ethics and morality. For her careful translations from the German, thanks to bilingual friend Wanda Benning.

The author appreciates the thorough critical review prepared by Dr. Robert Broussard, clinical psychologist and family therapist in Topsfield, Massachusetts. Thanks to Julie Jackson at Merrimack College in North Andover, Massachusetts, for arranging his involvement. Thanks also to Ann Hickman for her practical assessment of the young adult viewpoint and to Dr. Alvin Goldfarb, president and CEO of the AWARE Foundation, for his prompt and targeted advice. Dr. Jack Davis, a physician in private practice in Kalispell, Montana, shared his wit and wisdom. His review of the manuscript is the least I have to thank him for.

Thanks also to editor Amy Shields for expanding the series and believing in its author. And, as always, infinite gratitude to Lloyd for being Lloyd and to Ann for being Ann.

FOREWORD

The truth is rarely pure and never simple •
• OSCAR WILDE •

This book began with the collection of questions about sex and sexuality from middle school and high school students. Unlike other books in this series that dealt with such topics as food and skin, getting questions was difficult. Some questions were silly, embarrassed, or obscene. Some papers were blank. Some schools and teachers who had been eager to help in the past chose not to participate this time.

Nonetheless, as time went on, more and more questions came in from serious and thoughtful young adults. They are answered here one by one, with a lot of facts and a few (I hope) well-supported opinions. My favorite question, however, was too good to relegate to a single chapter. It just had to provide the framework for the entire book. It came from a student in Chesapeake, Virginia.

"Sex? What's the big deal?"

That seemed the most fundamental question of all and one that deserved a serious answer. As I usually do in responding to questions, I turned to the data that science can provide and found some answers reported in *Jet* magazine. A survey sponsored by Columbia University and the National Institutes of Health asked people to rate the importance of sex and other factors in their lives. Among 500 adults, 82 percent judged a satisfying sex life as "important" or "very important." Sex came in fourth behind loving family relationships (99 percent), financial security (98 percent), and religion (86 percent).[1]

On such an important subject, we are too often silent at home, at church, and in school classrooms. If this book can break that silence—for even one reader—its purpose will have been achieved. Sex is as much a part of healthy human living as breathing. There's no room for nervous twitters or uncomfortable laughter when the subject comes up. Each of us lives because of sex, and sexuality lives in us. Writes author and sex educator Debra Haffner: "Sexuality is about who we are as men and women, and not about what we do with a part of our bodies. . . . We are sexual beings from birth to death."[2]

And that's what this book is about.

A NOTE ABOUT AIDS

This book contains many questions and answers about sexually transmitted diseases, but questions about acquired immunodeficiency syndrome (AIDS) and the human immunodeficiency virus (HIV) are conspicuous in their absence. They have been omitted here not because they lack importance—AIDS is, after all, the most deadly of all sexually transmitted diseases—but because a book of this length and scope cannot begin to treat the subject in the depth it deserves.

Despite the publication of countless books and articles and despite 20 years of public education, too many people remain uninformed or misinformed about AIDS. A 1999 survey found that 40 percent of respondents believed that HIV can be transmitted via a public toilet (it can't), and about a third thought HIV could be transmitted while donating or giving blood (wrong again). Half of the respondents to three surveys believed they could contract HIV by sharing a drinking glass with someone who has the disease.[1] It's not true. HIV is spread when the blood, semen, or vaginal fluids of one person enter the body of another. That happens only during sexual contact and when IV drug users share unsterilized needles.

Dr. Gregory Herek at the University of California at Davis says, "A lot of Americans believe that any type of sex between two men can transmit HIV even when neither is infected with the virus."[2] That belief is incorrect. One person must be infected with the virus for another to get it. Still another misconception is that only homosexuals get AIDS. In truth, transmission between males and females is the fastest-growing cause of new AIDS cases, and mother-child transmission of HIV during pregnancy is an ever-growing crisis.

Because knowledge about HIV/AIDS can save lives, readers are advised to look beyond this volume for answers to their questions about AIDS. Interested readers are referred to some of the many excellent books on AIDS and HIV now available. My book *AIDS: Facts, Issues, Choices* (PPI Publishing, 1997) is a good place to start, and I especially recommend Barbara Brooker's *God Doesn't Make Trash* (Xlibris Corporation, 2000).

The history of the AIDS epidemic and extensive medical information are provided in *AIDS Doctors: Voices from the Epidemic: An Oral History* by Ronald Bayer and Gerald M. Oppenheimer (Oxford University Press, 2000). *The Amfar AIDS Handbook: The Complete Guide to Understanding HIV and AIDS* by Darrell Ward (Norton, 1998) is a comprehensive reference volume for those seeking in-depth knowledge. Teachers and health care providers will appreciate the lesson plans in *EveryBody: Preventing HIV and Other Sexually Transmitted Diseases among Young Teens* by Deborah Schoeberlein (Carbondale, CO: RAD Educational Programs, 2000).

CHAPTER ONE

THAT SHOULD
COME FIRST

*Each of us is a sexual individual, and that means
each of us is a unique conglomeration of sexual interests and
fantasies, turn-ons and turn-offs, orientations and behaviors,
things that we do and things that we don't do.*

• JAMES A. JOHNSON •

What Is
Sexuality?

Sometimes we think of sexuality as physical acts such as kissing, caressing, or having sexual intercourse. Human sexuality is, however, much more. While sexuality is rooted in biology, it goes far beyond the physical. It begins in gender identity. That's your basic concept of yourself as male or female. It's how you think the sexes are supposed to think, feel, and act in our society. Culture molds human sexuality. It's as important as the hormones that trigger sexual feelings.

Sexuality begins during prenatal life, long before an embryo has developed any sexual organs. The embryo's cells contain chromo-

A SEM (scanning electron micrograph) of X and Y chromosomes. Inside the nucleus, most males have one X and one Y chromosome. Most females have two Xs.

somes (packages of genes) that control sex. Most cells contain 22 matched pairs of somatic (meaning body) chromosomes. Another pair, the sex chromosomes, may be the same or different. Most females have a pair of sex chromosomes identified by the letter X. Most males have an X chromosome and a Y chromosome.

In the early weeks of development, the embryo's tiny brain triggers the manufacture of sex hormones. Hormones are chemicals made by one organ that affect another. If a Y chromosome is present, larger amounts of the male hormone testosterone are made. Testosterone causes the gonads (sex organs) to develop as the male testicles (or testes) and penis. If little testosterone is present, the embryo develops as a female. The gonadal tissue becomes the ovaries. Other female internal structures, including the uterus and Fallopian tubes, form. These internal structures will make childbearing possible in the future. The external female genitals, or vulva, also develop.

The gonads soon begin producing hormones on their own. The ovaries make the "female" hormones estrogen and progesterone, as well as the "male" hormone testosterone (but in much smaller amounts). The testicles make testosterone in large quantities and estrogen in smaller amounts. (The opposite-sex hormones are more than curiosities. They play an important role in sexual development. Testosterone in females stimulates sexual interest and arousal, while estrogen in males is vital to the maturation of sperm.)

The sex hormones also affect the brain, as do the environment in the uterus before birth, and the physical and social environment after birth. Together, the genes we inherit, our hormones, and our environment account for the differences in how each of us develops and expresses our sexuality.

Many forces influence human sexuality, sometimes in opposing ways. For example, tight and revealing clothing styles, sexually suggestive music, and fantasy sexual themes in movies promote sexual risk taking. At the same time, cautious advice from real-life parents, teachers, and church leaders urge restraint. Friends can send mixed signals, too. As one high school girl explained, "They say you're a coward if you don't have sex and a slut if you do. How can I win?"

In our society, many believe that the most important influence on sexuality is—or should be—the family. From our families, we first derive our gender identity. What we believe about appropriate male or female behavior comes first from the role models our parents provide. Sometimes, sadly, family communication breaks down. Parents may be ill, unavailable, or confused about sex. Their children may feel embarrassed or afraid to ask questions. In such cases, young adults have others they can turn to. They can look toward individuals or organizations in school or the community to help them reach sexual maturity. That means achieving four goals:

1. feeling good about the body and its functions;
2. recognizing and valuing sexual feelings;
3. making responsible decisions about sexual activities;
4. participating in caring relationships that nurture respect for both self and others.

What Organs Produce Sexual Feelings?

While the term genitals describes the sexual organs of both males and females, the only organ truly responsible for sexual feelings is the brain. It receives nerve impulses from many parts of the body. It interprets those messages as sexual interest, desire, arousal, or pleasure.

In males, the penis is the main source of sexual messages to the brain. In females, it's the clitoris. In both sexes, the neck, ears, lips, palms, forearm, anus, inner thigh, and popliteal space (behind the knee) are also sensitive areas, as may be the breasts, particularly around the nipples. Individual humans vary, however, and touches that stimulate one person may fail to arouse another.

Because the brain is the real sex organ, sexual feelings can occur without any physical stimulation. Pictures of sexual acts can do it, as can thoughts, fantasies, imagination,

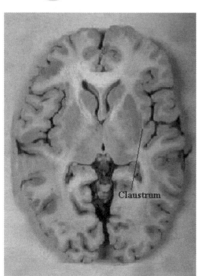
Claustrum

The claustrum inside the brain is the true sex organ.

and daydreams. In France, scientists showed sexually explicit videos to nine men. The researchers used an imaging technique called PET (positron emission tomography) to take pictures of what was going on inside the men's brains. The brain region called the claustrum showed the greatest increase in activity. That area specializes in emotion and motivation.

What and Where Are the Male Sex Organs?

The end of the penis is called the glans, or head. In most men, this is the area most sensitive to sexual touch. In uncircumcised men, it lies underneath a sheath of retractable skin called the prepuce, or foreskin. When the penis is not erect, the foreskin covers the glans. The foreskin pushes back during erection, masturbation, or before intercourse. In men who have been circumcised (usually in infancy), the foreskin is absent.

On the underside of the penis lies a ridge of tissue, the raphe, which extends the length of the shaft. The coronal ridge is the area where the glans and the shaft meet. On the underside of that ridge lies the V-shaped frenum, or frenulum. The shaft of the penis is made of spongy tissue packed with many blood vessels. Veins are easy to see on the outside. During sexual arousal (or sometimes for no apparent reason at all) blood collects in the penis. The spongy tissues fill with fluid, causing the penis to harden and rise. This is an erection.

The urethral meatus is the opening at the tip of the penis. It is the end of the tube, the urethra, which carries urine from the body. It also carries semen, but not both at the same time. Semen is the mixture of fluid and sperm cells propelled from a man's body when he ejaculates, usually during sexual climax, or orgasm.

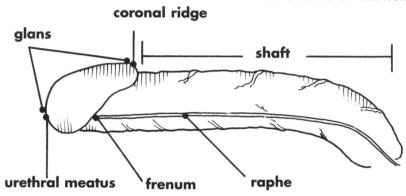

glans

coronal ridge

shaft

urethral meatus

frenum

raphe

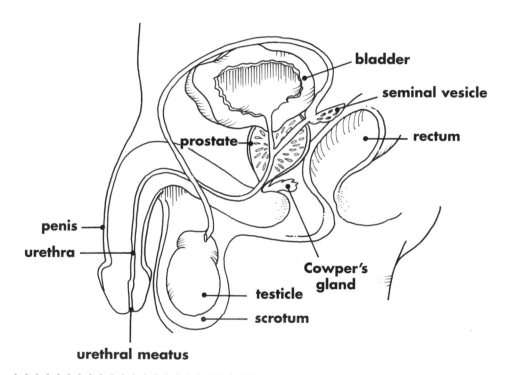

bladder

seminal vesicle

rectum

prostate

Cowper's gland

penis

urethra

testicle

scrotum

urethral meatus

The structures that make sperm cells are visible on the outside of the male body. They are the testicles, encased in their sac of wrinkled, darkened skin, the scrotum. Sperm cells made in the testicles travel through a series of tubes on their way to the urethral meatus. Along the way, fluid is added from the Cowper's gland, the seminal vesicles, and the prostate gland.

What and Where Are the Female Sex Organs?

In the female, the term vulva includes all the externally visible structures. The mound where pubic hair grows is the mons, or mons pubis. The folds that surround the vagina are the labia. The area of skin that lies between the vaginal opening and the anus is the perineum.

The focal area for sexual pleasure in a female is the clitoris. This button of tissue lies toward the front of the labia, just forward of the urinary opening. A hood of skin covers the clitoris. During sexual arousal, the clitoris fills with blood and hardens in much the same way as does the male penis. The clitoris contains about 8,000 nerve endings. That's about twice as many as the male penis.[1]

Before they become sexually active, some girls are confused about the urethra (through which urine leaves the body) and the vagina. In females, they are different openings. They do not join in any way. The urethral opening, which is smaller, lies in front of the vagina. Sexual pleasure arises from stimulation of the clitoris and also (in some females more than others) from pressure on the walls of the vagina.

Tissues in the vagina secrete lubricating fluids that allow easy entry by the penis during sexual intercourse. As intercourse ends, the male

SEX ORGANS OF THE HUMAN FEMALE

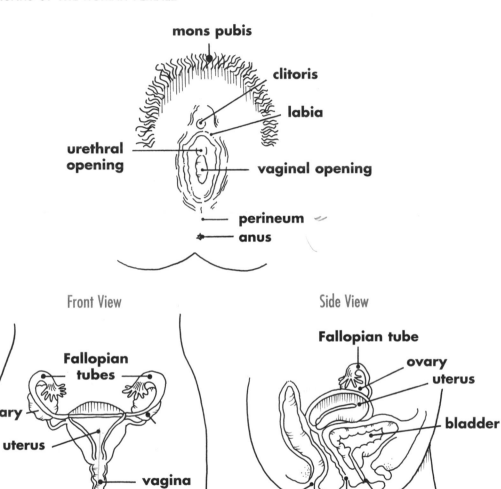

mons pubis

clitoris

labia

urethral opening

vaginal opening

perineum

anus

Front View

Fallopian tubes

ovary

uterus

vagina

Side View

Fallopian tube

ovary

uterus

bladder

anus

vagina

urethral opening

ejaculates sperm cells into the vagina. From there, they swim into the uterus and Fallopian tubes. If a sperm cell unites with an egg cell from the female ovary, pregnancy begins.

What Is Puberty?

Puberty isn't an event. It's a process, and it takes several years. It's the time when making a baby becomes possible. It involves the production of viable sperm cells in males and the release of egg cells in females. Boys usually know that puberty is happening because they have their first ejaculation. Often this occurs during sleep and is called a nocturnal emission, or "wet dream." Girls know they have entered puberty when they have their first menstrual period. Menstruation is the shedding of an unfertilized egg and the lining of the uterus. It happens when the egg released that month from the ovary has not been fertilized by a sperm cell. The monthly shedding of the lining makes way for the formation of a new lining and a possible pregnancy in the next month.

Puberty actually begins long before these first physical signs appear. It starts in a small gland at the base of the brain called the pituitary. Sometime well before the teen years, this gland releases gonadotropic hormones. These hormones trigger the enlargement and maturation of testicles in males and ovaries in females. These hormones also stimulate the testicles and ovaries to produce sex hormones of their own. These secondary hormones are the ones that prompt the development and release of mature, viable sperm and egg cells. Puberty does not end with the formation of sex cells. Changes in body shape, composition, and function continue throughout young adult life.

Physical and sexual development are not the only changes between ages 10 and 20. Society requires young adults to learn to live independently from parents and to identify and pursue a career goal. The teen years are also the time when the spiritual, emotional, and intellectual bases of an adult self-image form. The notion of self that forms during puberty endures for a lifetime.

I've Started to Notice Some Pretty Foal Smells Coming From My Armpits and Genitals. Is That Normal?

Yes. The human body has two kinds of sweat glands. The eccrine are distributed over the entire body. They are active at all times of life. They help regulate body temperature and excrete waste products. The second type, the apocrine glands, are inactive in childhood. They start to work during puberty when levels of sex hormones increase. They empty into hair follicles mostly in the armpits and groin. These glands produce a thick, colored fluid that contains a complex mixture of fats, water, and proteins. Perspiration from the apocrine glands is odorless, but when bacteria break it down chemically, odors are produced. That makes underarm deodorants and antiperspirants popular in our culture.

Another substance that collects under the foreskin of the male and inside the labial folds of females is called smegma. Smegma looks white, thick, and curdish, a little like ricotta cheese. It's a complex mixture of oily secretions and cast-off body cells. It serves to lubricate the genital area, but can become smelly if too much accumulates. Males should never force back a tight foreskin to clean out smegma. A regular bath or shower is usually sufficient to clean away the excess.

Human sexual response moves through several stages. A touch, a kiss, a thought, or a fantasy may be enough to get it started. The pupils of the eyes dilate, and the heart beats faster. In women, blood engorges the walls of the vagina and the clitoris. The folds around the vagina and the clitoris swell. The interior walls of the vagina secrete a fluid that moistens and lubricates them. The outer muscles of the vagina contract. Breasts swell and nipples harden, especially if touched.

In men, increased blood flow causes the penis to swell. It gets bigger, darker in color, and rises up and away from the body. The testicles pull toward the body and the scrotum tightens. As in the female, breasts and nipples may harden and become more sensitive. Muscles tighten though the whole pelvic area, giving a full, tense feeling.

If sexual activity ceases at this point, these reactions diminish and disappear. If stimulation continues, the outer walls of the vagina swell even more and get darker, and the outer segment of the vagina tightens. Inside the body, the uterus rises. In some women, the clitoris pulls in and under its hood of skin.

In males, the penis grows fully erect, and the testicles pull even closer to the body. Many males emit some pre-ejaculate fluid. In both sexes, breasts swell more and nipples become harder. Muscle tension increases around the lower abdomen and anus. At this stage, many people develop a redness of the skin, particularly around the midriff. This is called the "sex flush."

With the peak of sexual excitement may come orgasm. The heart pounds and blood pressure rises. In the female, the muscular walls of the vagina contract rhythmically. The uterus inside the body contracts, too. In the male, semen flows into the urethra. A valve that lies between the bladder and the urethra closes so that no urine can be released. The muscles of the penis contract, propelling semen from the urethral meatus.

After orgasm or when sexual activity ceases, the body returns to normal. Heart rate drops. Breathing slows. The body may be wet with perspiration. Blood leaves the genital area, and the swelling of the penis and clitoris subsides. The body relaxes. Immediately after ejaculation, most males cannot become aroused again for some period of time. Many females are, however, capable of additional sexual activity after orgasm.

How Do Males and Females Masturbate, and Is It OK?

Masturbation is sexual arousal by massaging the genitals, either with hands and fingers or with some object. Usually, masturbation is self-stimulation, carried out alone and in private. However, two or more people can masturbate together—rubbing each other's genitals—and some people become sexually aroused watching others masturbate.

Many young people discover masturbation by accident. It's natural for a boy to stimulate himself sexually when turning over in bed or holding his penis to urinate. Because the clitoris lies within the folds of the labia, girls are often later in learning how to masturbate. Their first experience may come in the shower, when the stream of water produces pleasurable feelings, or during insertion of a tampon, when the folds of the labia rubbing against the clitoris produce a pleasant sensation.

Masturbation is a normal, natural, and pleasurable part of sexuality for both sexes. There is nothing wrong with masturbation, and the only way it can harm you is if you feel guilty or worried about it—and then it's the guilt and worry that hurt, not the masturbation.

If you masturbate, know that you are not alone. Among young adults, some 95 percent of boys and 75 percent of girls, masturbate.[2] Most adults masturbate, too, whether single, married, or involved with a sex partner.

While you need not masturbate if you don't want to, most experts think masturbation is both healthy and beneficial. It serves to release sexual tensions, and may help young adults postpone sexual intercourse until they feel emotionally ready. For people of all ages, masturbation is a practical alternative to sexual intercourse. It poses zero risk of pregnancy or disease if practiced alone. If practiced with a partner, the risk of pregnancy remains low, but care must be taken to avoid transmission of diseases—as might occur, for example if semen containing the AIDS virus came in contact with broken skin on the hand.

Masturbation is good preparation for a sexual relationship. Boys and men often have a problem with ejaculating too quickly, before their female partner is aroused or satisfied. Through masturbation, men can learn to sustain their erection and delay orgasm. Females often feel disappointed in partnered sex because they do not become sufficiently aroused. Through masturbation, a girl can discover what stimulation heightens her sexual pleasure and produces orgasm. She can then communicate her needs to her partner.

Is It Possible to Masturbate Too Much? No. If your body is not prepared for stimulation of the genital area, it will simply fail to respond. Forget the claims that masturbation will make you grow hair in your palms or go blind. It will not. It doesn't cause mental illness, dark circles under the eyes, muscle weakness, pimples, or any other side effect. Like other sexual behaviors, masturbation should be a safe, guilt-free, and private matter. Whether and how often you masturbate are your business and no one else's.

One word of caution. Masturbation with objects can be dangerous. Boys should not listen to their friends who suggest stimulation of the penis with such devices as vacuum cleaner hoses. Girls risk infections if they insert cucumbers, bananas, or other objects into the vagina. It is best to masturbate with clean hands. They are both safe and effective.

On TV, Sex Seems So Wonderful, and Everyone Is "Doing It." Am I Missing Out?

Writes Thomas Hearn Jr. of Wake Forest University, "The only place love is free and sex is safe is in the media."[3]

Sex in film and TV entertainment is just that . . . entertainment. The average young adult in the United States views nearly 14,000 sexual references, acts, or implications on television annually. Only 175 of those make any reference to abstinence (not having sex) or contraception (preventing pregnancy). In one study, investigators reviewed 88 TV scenes of intercourse. Not one included even a passing reference to sexual risks or responsibilities.[4]

The entertainment industry peddles fantasy, not fact. Real-life sexual intercourse is seldom the ecstatic and perfectly choreographed ballet of bodies shown on television or the big screen. It's awkward, sweaty, a little embarrassing, sometimes uncomfortable, and often downright humorous. Couples in long-term sexual relationships say that it takes months, even years, to develop the kind of intimacy that TV and film stars appear to achieve with their first and every encounter.

Are Young People Having Sex Earlier Than They Used To?

The answer depends on how many years you look back. During most of the twentieth century, the U.S. average age of first intercourse fell, while the number of young people having their first intercourse before the age of 13 rose. But, in the 1990s, that trend reversed. More young adults chose to postpone sexual intercourse.[5]

In 1999 experts estimated that 12.2 percent of males and 4.4 percent of females had sexual intercourse (usually defined as penis in vagina) before their 13th birthday.[6] That was a drop of 0.5 percent compared with 1993.[7] At the same time the numbers of high school students who have never had sex increased. (See the chart on page 28.) In recent years, teens have been improving their record in protecting themselves against unwanted pregnancies and sexually transmitted diseases such as AIDS.

What's the Difference Between Homosexual, Heterosexual, and Bisexual?

These terms describe sexual preferences and partnerships, often called sexual orientation. People who feel attracted to, or prefer having sex with, a member of their same gender are said to be homosexual. Female homosexuals are often termed lesbians. Males are often called gay. Heterosexuals have male-female sexual attractions and intercourse. Another name for heterosexual is "straight." Bisexuals are said to be attracted to members of both their own and the opposite sex.

In reality, the distinctions among people are not as clear-cut as the words might suggest. One fourth of American men, for example, say they have had sexual experience with another male, but a much

HIGH SCHOOL STUDENTS WHO HAVE NEVER HAD SEXUAL INTERCOURSE*

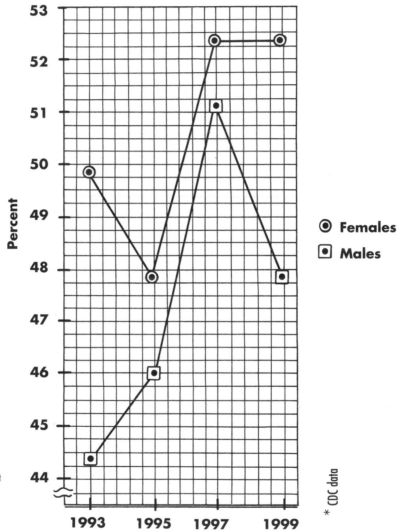

The percentage of high school students who have never had sex is higher in 1999 than in 1993.

* CDC data

smaller number identify themselves as homosexual.[8] One study used desire, self-reported preference, and behavior as three different ways to define homosexuality and bisexuality. Using all three characteristics, the researchers estimated 2.4 percent of men and 1.3 percent of women are homosexual or bisexual. If only one characteristic is used as a measure, 10.1 percent of men and 8.6 percent of women qualify.[9]

Are Attitudes Toward Homosexuality Changing?

It appears so. Between 1988 and 1998, more people—both men and women—reported same-gender sex partners within the previous year.[10]

Two explanations for that trend make sense, and both involve growing social acceptance.

PERCENT REPORTING A SEX PARTNER OF THE SAME GENDER IN THE PAST YEAR*

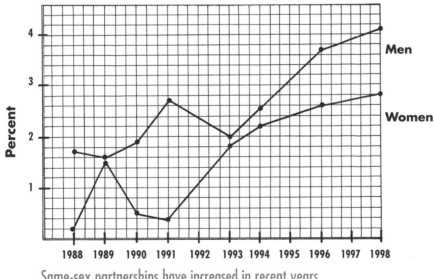

Same-sex partnerships have increased in recent years.

* Data from Butler, A. "Trends in Same-Gender Partnering, 1988–1998, *The Journal of Sex Research*, November 4, 2000, pp. 333–343.

First, the number of people having same-gender partners may have risen because people felt freer to act on their same-gender attractions. Or the numbers may have remained the same, but more people are now willing to admit same-sex partnerships.

Still, people with same-gender sexual preferences may face prejudice and discrimination. While some religions value all people, regardless of their sexual orientation, others condemn homosexuality as "unnatural" or "a sin." In a survey sponsored by the conservative political action organization People for the American Way, more than half the respondents said that sexual relations between members of the same sex was "always wrong."[11] Over time, more people may come to understand what biologists have known for centuries: Sexual expression takes many different forms among all living things, including humans.

How Can I Know If I Am Gay, Lesbian, Bisexual, or Straight?

If you feel attracted to a member of your same sex, does that mean you are homosexual? If you engage in sexual activity with a same-sex partner, does that make you gay or lesbian? Not necessarily, say UCLA researchers Letitia Peplau and Linda Garnets. "Sexual orientation [is] not fixed and universal, but rather highly variable across time and place."[12]

Sexual orientation is a process, not a product. Researcher Lisa Diamond interviewed 80 lesbian, bisexual, and undecided women. Their ages ranged from 16 to 23. She talked with them several times over two years. She learned that, while their sexual attractions remained fairly stable, half of them changed their stated sexual identity. She also found that many were attracted to both sexes, but unwill-

STAGES IN THE DEVELOPMENT OF HOMOSEXUAL IDENTITY[13]

STAGE	APPROXIMATE AGE	ATTITUDES/BEHAVIORS
Sensitization	Younger than 14	Feeling of being different from same-sex peers
Identity Confusion	14–16	Attraction to same-sex; lack of interest in opposite sex; turmoil, confusion, and anxiety
Identity Assumption	21–23	Contact with homosexuals, self-identification as a homosexual, sexual experimentation
Commitment	(before age 28)	Open same-sex relationship; disclosure of homosexual identity to family and friends; incorporation of sexual identity into all aspects of life.

ing to label themselves bisexual. Half of the women changed their sexual identity more than once. One fourth of self-identified lesbians had sex with men sometime during the study period.[14]

Many young people who struggle to define their sexual orientation think that they are alone. They feel isolated from others who seem so secure in their heterosexual orientation. The facts run counter to that view. One survey in Seattle, for example, collected data from more than 8,000 high school students. Nearly 5 percent considered themselves gay, lesbian, or bisexual. Another 4 percent said they weren't sure.[15] Added together, that's 1 in every 11 people—not a majority, but no small minority either.

Margaret Blythe of the Indiana University School of Medicine says it's OK to feel attractions to people of your own sex, opposite sex, or both. Don't jump to conclusions, she advises, and don't be in a hurry to label yourself. Your sexual identity will emerge over time as you grow into adulthood.[16] If your feelings make you anxious or guilty, talk about them with an adult you trust—a parent, counselor, teacher, or doctor. That friend and confidant should help you understand your sexuality without making you feel ashamed or afraid.

If, in later life, you decide that you are homosexual or bisexual, you should be able to make that choice without fear of prejudice from your friends, co-workers, or family. That acceptance is not always easy, because some people view homosexuality or bisexuality as unnatural or wrong. Only by facing those biases head-on can we hope to create a society that is accepting and supportive of human sexuality in all its forms.

Can Homosexuals Go Straight If They Want To?

Expect disagreement if you ask that one in public.

The answer from both the American Psychological Association and the American Psychiatric Association is "no." Homosexuality is not a disease. It requires no "treatment." Neither is it a conscious decision that can be—or needs to be—reversed. The American Psychological Association says:

> Human beings cannot choose to be either gay or straight. Sexual orientation emerges for most people in early adolescence without any prior sexual experience. Although we can choose whether to act on our feelings, psychologists do not consider sexual orientation to be a conscious choice that can be voluntarily changed.[17]

Nevertheless, some organizations and individuals claim to be able to change gays into straights. "Reorientation," "reparative," or "conversion" therapy offers prayer and group counseling to people who want to change. Some seek change because they feel that their sexual orientation conflicts with their religion. Others are emotionally distressed, feeling that their lives are out of control. Although scientific evidence is thin, testimonials from ex-gays sometimes claim success. "The groups . . . give you the time to get away from sex long enough to start thinking a little more clearly. It was a big part of the recovery process for me," one advocate said.[18]

"The potential risks of 'reparative' therapy are great: including depression, anxiety, and self-destructive behavior," says the American Psychiatric Association. Mental health professionals fear that attempts to change orientation may fuel self-hatred or reinforce societal prejudices against homosexuality. "There is no published scientific evidence supporting the efficacy of 'reparative' therapy as a treatment to change one's sexual orientation," the Association stated in 1998.[19]

Three years later, Robert Spitzer, a psychiatrist at Columbia University, presented findings that cautiously questioned that view. Spitzer interviewed 200 people who said they had once been homosexual, but had changed because of conversion therapy. Nearly two thirds of the men and not quite half the women reported that they felt heterosexual attractions after the therapy that they had rarely or never felt before. Some of those whose orientation did not change—but who gave up homosexual behavior—said they felt better emotionally.[20]

It took Spitzer 16 months to find his subjects, recruited mostly through religious organizations. He believes their experience is rare. "I don't do this kind of therapy, and I am skeptical about the results," he says.[21] While he opposes pressuring people, he thinks gays and lesbians "should have the right to explore their heterosexual potential."[22]

About one in every 60 individuals has some genetic, physical, or hormonal complication that affects sexual identity and development.[23] Mild cases of unusual genitals—such as testicles that don't descend from the abdomen into the scrotum (as normally happens before birth)—occur about once in every 100 infants. Surgery is usually performed on undescended testicles, because leaving them in the abdomen increases the risk of testicular cancer in later life. Other minor variations in the genitals need no treatment or correction.

More unusual—about 1 in every 3,000 births—are cases of "intersex" individuals with "ambiguous genitals." Intersex conditions may include an enlarged clitoris, a small penis, an inadequate vagina, or underdeveloped testicles. Sometimes a female with ovaries has male-like external genitals. Rarely, newborns have both ovaries and testicles. In certain cases, the child's biological sex cannot be determined from external appearance.

A hormonal imbalance during development in the womb is often the cause. One such condition, called CAH (congenital adrenal hyperplasia), is an enzyme deficiency of the adrenal glands. It causes the adrenals to produce too much of the male hormone testosterone. CAH can cause enlargement of the penis or clitoris.

Another hormonal condition, AIS (androgen insensitivity syndrome), makes fetal cells unable to respond to male hormones. An infant with AIS may have normal-looking female genitals on the outside, but testicles on the inside. "It's important to understand that ambiguous genitals are not an oddity of nature. These are simply parts of the body that are only partially developed," says Donald Zimmerman, an endocrinologist at the Mayo Clinic.[24]

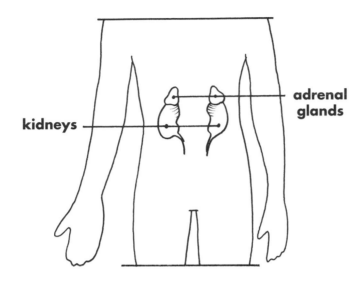

kidneys

adrenal glands

The adrenal glands lie above the kidneys. They make testosterone in both males and females.

In the past, doctors routinely performed surgery to "assign" an external sexual identity to an individual or to "correct" the appearance of the genitals. Recent research calls this practice into question. Researchers Catherine Minto and Sarah Creighton in London reported that most girls who had vaginas surgically created in infancy needed additional major surgery as adults in order to have sexual intercourse. They found that one fourth of girls who had clitoral reductions could not achieve orgasm in adult life.[25] Johns Hopkins scientists found that boys born with an unusually small penis mature better if raised as males. For these and other reasons, Zimmerman suggests, "it might be better to wait to let intersex children grow up to decide their own gender."[26]

What Do
Transgender
and Transsexual
Mean?

Gender identity is a person's internal sense of being male or female. In most people, gender identity matches biological sex. Males feel at ease being men, and females feel comfortable being women. A few individuals, however, grow to adulthood with an ever-increasing sense of being trapped in the wrong body. Their physical sex and their gender identity conflict. The term transgender refers to people who feel, look, or behave in ways typically associated with the opposite sex.

"Gender dysphoria" (unhappiness about one's apparent gender as defined by outward appearances or anatomy) is not uncommon. Some individuals grow distressed enough with their physical sex to want to change it. If they do—through surgery and hormone treatments—they are termed transsexual. Worldwide estimates suggest about 1 in every 12,000 people is a male to female transsexual. One in every 30,000 is a female to male transsexual.[27]

Can a Boy Be
Raised as a
Girl, or Vice
Versa?

Not a good idea.

William C. Reiner, a psychologist and urologist at Johns Hopkins Hospital studied 27 children who were born without a penis. All had male genes and male sex hormones. Twenty-five of the 27 were sexually "reassigned" at birth. Their testicles were removed, and their parents tried to raise them as girls.

Reiner says the children, ages 5 to 16 in his study, enjoyed the typical male rough and tumble style of play; and 14 declared themselves to be boys, one as young as the age of five.[28] "They seem to be quite capable of telling who they are," Reiner says.[29] The two boys who were not surgically altered at birth are psychologically better adjusted and developmentally more like other young males, Reiner notes.

"When the brain has been masculinized by exposure to testosterone, it is kind of useless to say to this individual, 'You're a girl,'" says physician Marianne Legato of Columbia University. "It is the impact of testosterone that gives males the feelings that they are men."[30]

Sexual Orientation: Is It in the Genes?

. . . . .

I hope the 21st century sees an end to the nature-nurture argument. We need to move forward and investigate how nature and culture interact.

HELEN FISHER

. . . . .

Sexual orientation refers to an individual's erotic desire for a member of the same sex (homosexual), opposite sex (heterosexual), or both sexes (bisexual). Is it a product of the environment, scientists want to know—something learned or triggered by social forces? Or is sexual orientation inborn, a product of the genes?

Genes are bits of DNA strung like beads along the 46 (usually) chromosomes that function inside the nucleus of most human cells. Genes control what proteins cells make and what those proteins do. Every human characteristic is genetic in the sense that DNA controls all life processes. But complex behavioral traits like sexual orientation aren't the products of a single gene pair. Multiple factors

interact. So, the question becomes not whether sexual orientation is genetic ("nature"), or environmental ("nurture"). It's obviously both. What researchers want to know is how large a role each plays in shaping an individual's sexual preferences.

One attempt to answer the question was reported in 1991, when J. Michael Bailey and Richard Pillard reported their studies of pairs of men: identical twins raised together; fraternal (not-identical) twins raised together; and men with adopted brothers. They determined whether one or both men in each pair were homosexual.[31]

Their findings indicated a possible genetic link. Identical twins, who share exactly the same genes, were

RELATIONSHIP	RATE OF HOMOSEXUALITY FOR BOTH
Identical Twins	52% (29 of 56)
Fraternal Twins	22% (12 of 54)
Adopted Brothers	11% (6 of 57)

shared genetic tendency, as expected. Their results indicated what Bailey and Pillard called a "moderate inheritance of sexual orientation." Two years later, a similar study of lesbian women showed similar results.[32]

Dean Hamer, a molecular geneticist at the National Institutes of Health, became interested in the biology of sexual orientation. He noticed that some family trees suggested an X-linked pattern of inheritance. That is, homosexual men were showing up frequently among the sons and grandsons of certain women. Boys

more likely to both be homosexual than fraternal twins, who share half their genes (just as siblings born at different times do). Adopted brothers, who are unrelated, showed no

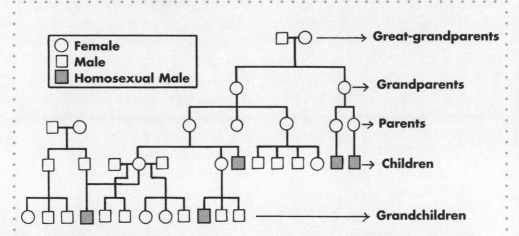

A family tree showing possible inheritance of homosexuality through the maternal (female) line. Notice how many homosexual sons and grandsons appear among the descendants of the sisters and female cousins shown on the Parents line.

Adapted from Michael Cummings, *Human Heredity* (Pacific Grove, CA: Brooks-Cole, 2000).

get their X chromosome from their mothers. Therefore, Hamer reasoned, some males might inherit their homosexuality in genes carried on the X chromosome.

To test his hypothesis, Hamer set out to find linkages between certain sequences of genes and homosexuality. Linkages are groups of genes inherited together on one chromo-some—in this case, the X chromosome. Hamer recruited 40 pairs of homosexual brothers whose family history showed homosexuality on the mother's side of the family. He analyzed their DNA. He looked for pieces of DNA that all or most of the men might have in common. If he found one, he reasoned, that piece might contain the genes that predispose for homosexuality.

Hamer and his team found a shared DNA segment. Of the 40 pairs of men, 33 shared a set of five markers. The markers were located near the end of the long arm of the X chromosome in a region named Xq28.

Hamer did not call Xq28 the "gay gene." He warned that this one site couldn't explain homosexual orientation. He noted that, in some families, the inheritance seemed to concentrate on the father's side of the family. And, seven of the pairs he studied did not have the markers. Hamer concluded that homosexuality arises from the interaction of a variety of factors, both genetic and environmental.[33]

Hamer's work has been criticized for several reasons. Some say Hamer

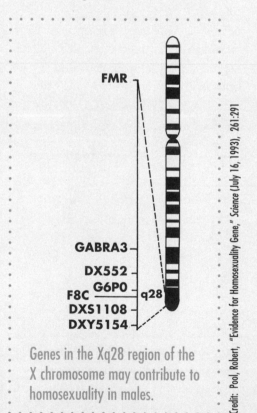

FMR

GABRA3
DX552
G6PO
F8C — q28
DXS1108
DXY5154

Genes in the Xq28 region of the X chromosome may contribute to homosexuality in males.

Credit: Pool, Robert, "Evidence for Homosexuality Gene," *Science* (July 16, 1993), 261:291

used too few subjects to allow valid conclusions. He worked only with gay men. Lesbians and bisexuals were excluded from his study. Hamer did not look for the Xq28 markers of the heterosexual brothers of the gay men he studied. If they had them too, then the markers' presence would mean nothing. Others point out that he accepted the word of his subjects regarding their homosexual orientation. Thus, the characteristic he was studying was not well defined. And because he sought out families where two sons were homosexual, his selection of participants may have exaggerated the influence of genes.

Still, the notion that DNA may direct sexual orientation is too intriguing for scientists to ignore. Some confirmation for Hamer's work has come, not from human studies, but from laboratory experiments with *Drosophila*, the lowly fruit fly. In 1995, Ward Odenwald and Shang-Ding Zhang at the National Institutes of Health transplanted a single gene into male fruit flies. The gene was one that normally affects only eye color and certain brain activities, but they transplanted it in such a way that it went to work in every cell. The result was male flies that preferred mating with other male flies.

Nothing, alas, is ever simple. The genetically altered flies mated with females when surrounded by large numbers of them, so technically they weren't gay, but bisexual. The gene had no effect on female flies either. The scientists were unable to produce lesbian *Drosophila*. Their experiments with the flies even demonstrated that environment can have an effect. When they mixed "straight" male fruit flies with the "gays," the heterosexuals hung around on the sidelines for a while as the gays mated. After a few hours, however, they joined in—becoming, for a time at least—as homosexual as the genetically altered flies.[34]

Elsewhere, other researchers have tried to repeat Hamer's studies of humans. Results have been mixed. In 1999, George Rice led a team of Canadian and California scientists who studied 52 pairs of gay brothers. They found no evidence of linkage of sexual orientation to Xq28.[35] In 2000, Kenneth Kendler of the Medical College of Virginia reported on his studies of nearly 1,600 twins and nearly as many non-twin siblings. Among 324 pairs of identical twins, 19 included at least one nonheterosexual twin. In 6 of those 19—nearly one third—both twins were gay or lesbian. Kendler and his team found nothing in the childhood or adult environments of the twins that predicted their shared orientation. They estimated the genetic contribution to sexual orientation at somewhere between 28 and 65 percent.[36]

Whatever the contribution of genes may be, all agree it's not total. Some gay men, for example, have an identical twin who is not gay. Since their genes are identical, something in their environment—perhaps even the environment inside the womb during development—may explain the difference. Other factors might include the mother's health habits or the effects of an unknown virus. The environment provided by family and community may also be important, although its influence is hard to study.

Anne Fausto-Sterling, a professor of biology at Brown University told *The New York Times*: "The best controlled studies . . . say that 50 percent of what goes into making a person homosexual is genetic. That means 50 percent is not. And while everyone is very excited about genes, we are clueless about the equally important nongenetic contributions."[37]

In the final analysis, the question may turn out to be pointless. To ask what part of any complex behavior is genetic or environmental is, according to Harvard psychologist Jerome Kagan, "like asking what proportion of a blizzard is due to cold temperature rather than humidity."[38]

Nevertheless, "We are still looking," George Rice says.[39]

CHAPTER TWO

QUESTIONS

YOUNG MEN ASK

Sex requires art, attention to details, and a devoted imagination.
• THOMAS MOORE •

Is My Penis Too Small?

If an Internet survey can be trusted, the average penis length is 6.5 inches (166 millimeters). The minimum is 2.4 inches (61 millimeters). The maximum is 11 inches (279 millimeters).[1] Anywhere in that range is probably normal, but soft (flaccid) length doesn't matter much anyway. Small penises grow more when they become erect than large ones do.

During puberty, the testicles and penis grow along with the rest of the body, but the rate of growth and eventual mature size vary among individuals. So do facial and pubic hair, depth of voice, and body build and musculature. Some boys look like men at 14, while others don't reach their full growth until they are 19 or 20.

Boys who develop later may feel inferior to more physically advanced young men. There's no reason to, and there's no way to speed up the process anyway. Genes control body development. Nothing anyone can do will change that. The best plan is to be patient and appreciate your healthy body. In time, the process of maturation evens out, and all adult male bodies turn out more or less the same.

Later-developing males also worry that they may not be able to please a woman during sexual intercourse. That's untrue also. Women can achieve sexual pleasure with a loving male partner of their choice, regardless of penis size. The female vagina is elastic and muscular. It automatically expands to fit a partner, assuming the woman is sufficiently aroused sexually. And, since only the outermost area of the vagina is sensitive to sexual stimulation, penile length has little effect on a woman's enjoyment.

Very rarely, slow penile growth truly is a medical concern. On the average, the male testicles produce between 7 and 10 milligrams of the male hormone testosterone in a 24-hour period.[2] If they don't, penile size may be affected. This medical condition, called hypogonadism (meaning small sex organs), occurs in about one in every 500 males.[3] It has many possible causes. An injury or malformation of the testicles may cause testosterone production to decline. Or, the pituitary gland in the brain may not send the necessary chemical messages to the testicles. The problem can arise from undescended testicles, drugs including cancer treatments, aging, glandular disorders, diseases of the immune systems, and even childhood diseases such as mumps. It may also occur among heavy drinkers of alcohol and men with certain serious long-term diseases such as diabetes.

Early detection is important, so if you are convinced your penis is abnormally small and your sexual development lagging, see a doctor. If laboratory tests confirm a low testosterone level in your blood, your doctor may prescribe pituitary hormones or testosterone replacement therapy. Lifestyle and dietary changes will help prevent the bone loss that goes along with low levels of hormone production.

I Get Erections at Embarrassing Times. Why, and How Can I Stop Them?

Many young men get erections at inopportune moments, such as when speaking in public or playing sports. In such cases, the stress or excitement of the moment may cause the erection, but sometimes erections spring up for no apparent reason. It's simply part of being young, male, and healthy.

If your erections are frequent and embarrassing, wear a snug jock strap to hold the penis against the body. And try a long shirt or sweatshirt that covers the groin. The problem is temporary. It will go away as you grow older.

I Don't Always Get an Erection When I Want To. Am I Normal?

Chances are, the answer is yes. Most men experience the inability to become erect—called erectile dysfunction, or impotence—at some times in their lives. Usually, the situation is temporary and easily resolved. In more serious and longer-lasting cases, it's accompanied by anxiety, depression, alcoholism, or unresolved problems with gender identity. It can be a side effect of prescription drugs or drug abuse. It may also be associated with certain heart, nerve, hormonal, and urinary disorders that a doctor can diagnose and treat. If the condition is persistent and distressing, a physician may prescribe drugs, counseling, or both.

The flow of blood into spongy tissues inside the penis causes the enlargement and hardening of an erection.

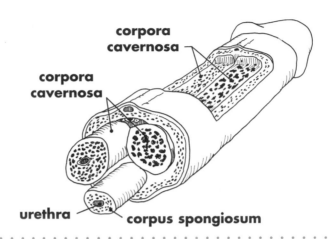

corpora cavernosa

corpora cavernosa

urethra

corpus spongiosum

My Penis Turns Purple When I Get an Erection. Is That Normal?

Yes. During an erection, blood collects in three spongy bodies of tissue in the penis. Two, the corpus cavernosa, run along the sides of the shaft. The third is located on the underside of the penis. It is the corpus spongiosum, and it surrounds the urethra. These structures begin inside the body, giving support to the penis and causing it to rise during sexual excitement. The infusion of blood into these tissues causes the color change. The penis may look brown, red, or purple.

I Have More (Less) Body Hair Than the Other Guys. Am I Normal?

Probably. The amounts of body hair men develop vary greatly among individuals and over the course of a lifetime. Male hormones surge during puberty and produce additional

• 46 •

body hair in the pubic area, armpits, face, chest, abdomen, and sometimes scalp. Some areas of scalp hair grow thicker under the influence of male hormones, while other areas may thin. But genes, ultimately, control hairiness. Two men may have identical hormone levels, but the hair follicles on one man's body grow large amount of hair, while those on the other man's do not. Changes in hairiness do not stop in adulthood. Men may develop heavier beards or more body hair well into middle age. Scalp hair loss can begin in the teen years in those genetically disposed to male pattern baldness.

A noticeable loss of body, armpit, and pubic hair—accompanied by a loss of interest in sex, breast enlargement, and erectile dysfunction—may be symptoms of a medical problem. Hair falling from the scalp in patches also demands a visit to the doctor.

Sometimes I Can Feel My Testicles Pulling Up Close to My Body. Is That Normal?

Inside the scrotum and between the two testicles lies a wall of muscle. The muscle pulls the testicles closer to the body. The movement is involuntary, especially in the cold or when danger threatens. It's a normal reflex, providing warmth and protection for the testicles.

Is It Possible to Get an Erection That Won't Go Away?

A painful erection that lasts for hours, even days, is called priapism. It is not associated with sexual thoughts or activities. It results from drugs or medical conditions. It develops because blood that flows into the penis cannot move out. Injected drugs used to treat erectile dysfunction can occasionally cause priapism. Medicines prescribed for depression are sometimes at fault. Blood diseases such as sickle-cell anemia and leukemia can be to blame, because they cause the blood to thicken and small blood vessels to clog.

Most men are quick to seek medical help for priapism. Treatment usually requires draining blood from the penis with a needle. Medications are available to treat the condition. They decrease blood flow into the penis. Sickle-cell anemia patients with priapism are usually treated by blood transfusion.

What Should I Do If I Notice a Lump or Swelling in My Scrotum?

The normal testicle measures about 1.5 inches (38 millimeters) long and about an inch (25 millimeters) wide.[4] One is usually slightly larger than the other. If yours are noticeably larger than that, or you notice any unusual lump or swelling, it's wise to see a doctor. A common reason for swelling in the scrotum in young boys is an accumulation of fluid around a testicle. This condition, called a hydrocele, is not dangerous, but it can cause discomfort. In some cases, surgery may be needed, but many cases clear up on their own.

A physician can, through examination and testing, rule out other possibilities, including:

- *testicular cancer.* Although cancer in a testicle is uncommon in the young, it can occur as early as age 15.
- *hernia.* A weakness of the muscular tissue of the lower abdomen may extend into the scrotum.

- *variocele*. A knot of distended veins in the sperm cord above a testicle.
- *an infection of the epididymis*. This bundle of tangled tubes sits atop the testicles. Sperm cells mature and are stored there.
- *orchitis*, or inflammation of a testicle. Orchitis may be painful and may occur as a result of infection.

One of My Testicles Harts, and It's Not Because of an Injury. Should I See a Doctor?

Yes. Each year, about one in every thousand men is diagnosed with epididymitis.[5] Epididymitis is an infection of the tube that carries sperm from the testicles to the penis. Besides pain, men may feel a swelling of the scrotum, frequent need to urinate or a feeling of needing to urinate, nausea, fever or chills, pain in the lower belly, or a discharge from the tip of the penis.

If this condition is suspected, the doctor will feel for a swelling in the tube. Laboratory tests may reveal a sexually transmitted infection. An infection by the normal intestinal bacterium *Escherichia coli* (also known as *E. coli*) can occur in young boys who have never had sex. It also happens to men who have anal intercourse with other men. The condition is treated with antibiotics.

Another possible reason for a sudden severe pain in a testicle is testicular torsion. Symptoms may include swelling of the scrotum, nausea and vomiting, pain in the lower belly, fever, or a frequent need to urinate. This emergency is more common among teens than among older men, usually affecting those between ages 12 and 18. It is not an infection. It is caused by an inborn abnormality of genital structure. It happens because the tunica vaginalis, which holds the testicle in place

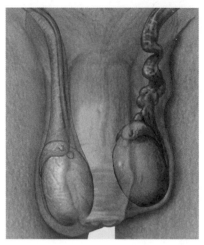
Testicular torsion is a serious medical emergency. Note how the sperm cord is twisted.

inside the scrotum, is attached too high. That allows the testicle to rotate. It can twist around the sperm cord, blocking blood flow to the testicle. That causes swelling and possibly rupture. While about 12 percent of males are born with this condition, only one in 4,000 males experiences testicular torsion.[6] It requires immediate emergency surgery—ideally within six hours after the onset of pain.

Will Excess Sperm Build Up in My Body If I Don't Ejaculate Often Enough?

No. Sperm survive in the epididymis for about four to six weeks. If they aren't ejaculated, they break down harmlessly. The chemical substances they are made from are reabsorbed and reused by the body.

What Is the Clear Liquid that Comes Out of My Penis Before Ejaculation?

It's a fluid from the Cowper's gland (also called bulbourethral gland) that helps clean the urethra and make conditions right for the survival of sperm cells. Because this fluid can contain sperm or disease-causing organisms, it can impregnate a female or pass disease along to a sexual partner. It's the reason why withdrawal (removing the penis from the vagina before ejaculation) cannot prevent pregnancy or disease.

This "pre-come" fluid is normal, but any other discharge from the penis is not. See a doctor if you notice fluid (other than urine) or pus coming from your penis.

What Is Premature Ejaculation?

Ejaculation happens too soon (prematurely) only if you and your sexual partner are unhappy about the timing. Men often worry that they "come" before their female partner is sufficiently aroused or satisfied. As you grow older, you'll be more able to bring your timing in tune with your partner's. Practicing delay while masturbating also helps slow the response.

My Breasts Are Rounded, Like a Girl's. What Should I Do?

Some 40 to 60 percent of males experience gynecomastia, or breast enlargement, at some time in their lives.[7] Newborn males normally have enlarged breasts, resulting from exposure to their mother's estrogen while in the womb. The breasts diminish in size in infancy. During puberty, however, about two thirds of young men experience some enlargement and tenderness of the breasts that may last for months.[8]

In overweight males, excess fatty tissue may be the reason. Although the cause for enlargement is not known in most other cases, it can be brought on by certain prescription drugs, liver disease, hormonal disorders, or marijuana use. Rarely, breast growth is associated with hypogonadism or an insufficiency of testosterone.

If breast tissue feels hard, if the nipple is deformed, or if it bleeds or exudes fluid, see a doctor immediately. If breast enlargement is a concern for appearance, liposuction can remove excess fat in the breast area or surgery can remove excess glandular tissue.

I Get "Jock Itch" Often. Is It a Sexually Transmitted Disease?

No. That red rash and chafed, itchy, irritated skin are caused by any of several kinds of fungi that live on the body surface. For food, the organisms use keratin, a protein that is abundant in skin, nails, and hair. Those fungi that cause jock itch are the same or similar to those that causes athlete's foot, and you can get an infection even if you are not playing sports. The fungi grow best in dark, damp places, so they thrive in the groin, inner thighs, and pubic and anal areas, especially if you perspire a lot in warm weather. Jock itch can be transmitted by human contact, but it need not be sexual.

To prevent jock itch, wear loose-fitting, all-cotton underwear and clothing, so the skin can dry after you sweat. Don't use other people's towels or wear other people's clothes. Avoid tight scratchy garments and synthetic materials. Go easy in the shower. Too much soap can make jock itch worse. Wash, but make sure to rinse and dry well. Over-the-counter powders

A SEM image of Epidermyo-phyton floccosum, the fungus that causes jock itch.

and lotions containing antifungal agents usually clear the condition quickly. Do not use athlete's foot medicines. They may be too harsh for the sensitive skin of the groin. If self-treatment fails, see a doctor for prescription medicine.

How Can I Tell If a Girl Wants to Have Sex?

Young men often mistake a girl's friendly smile or casual conversation for a sexual invitation. Marie Haselton and David Buss at the University of Texas at Austin surveyed more than 500 college students.[9] They asked volunteers to rate the level of sexual interest revealed by an act such as holding hands or complimenting appearance. They discovered that men overestimated women's sexual interest. When men were asked to imagine the actions as coming from their sisters, they were far more accurate in their ratings. So, picture that sweet smile as coming from your sister—not your date—and you'll get the right message. And always remember that "no" means "no."

Who Invented the Condom?

The inventor of the condom is unknown, but a sheath that covers and protects the penis goes back a long way. In ancient Egypt, men wore penis protectors not to prevent disease or pregnancy, but for shielding in war, as decoration, and to show social rank. In Japan, they wore a covering made of tortoise shell or horn. Condoms sewn from linen were used in the fifteenth century when an epidemic of syphilis swept Europe and Asia. By the eighteenth century, the English were making condoms by hand from the intestines of sheep.

A technician pours water into a condom during a press conference by a condom manufacturer.

How Are
Condoms
Made?

It might be said that the second-greatest technological breakthrough for human sexuality was Charles Goodyear's process for vulcanizing rubber. (The first has to be the birth control pill, which came along in 1960.) Goodyear invented the process in 1839.[10] For nearly a century after that, condoms were made by dipping forms in rubber cement. The condoms aged quickly and broke frequently, but they offered better protection than linen or sheepskin. In the 1930s, manufacturers developed an even better material, the natural latex from rubber trees.

Latex comes from plantations mostly in Malaysia, Thailand, Indonesia, Vietnam, and West Africa. Tapping latex trees is similar to tapping maple trees. A tool that resembles a corkscrew bores into the tree, and the latex drips out from the wound. Additives keep the latex chemically stable. Dried latex is used to manufacture rubber tires. Liquid latex is needed for making gloves, balloons, and condoms.

To make a condom, a mold (also called a former) is dipped into liquid latex. The condom is then dried, washed, and tested. Several different types of tests are available. In a "dry test" apparatus, an electrical current burns a hole in any weak spot—and the condom is, of course, rejected. A "wet test" device measures electrical conductivity between the inside and outside of the condom. Those with low resistance fail the test. Air testing inflates condoms, checking that they can withstand a certain amount of pressure without breaking.

Today, world production of condoms totals somewhere between eight and ten billion a year. Researchers think nearly twice that many are needed to offer our world population adequate protection against sexually transmitted diseases, including AIDS.[11]

Should I Use a Condom?

Yes, if you have any kind of sexual contact, you should. Condoms protect against pregnancy when used for penile-vaginal intercourse. They protect against the transmission of disease when used during anal, oral, or vaginal sex. Apparently, young adults are getting the message. Condom use is on the rise in the United States.

Why Do Condoms Fail?

Leaky or defective condoms are extremely rare. Failure usually results from improper storage and use. Too many guys carry a condom in their wallet or shoe for weeks or months, hoping to "get lucky." They don't, and the condom package gets torn, causing the contents to deteriorate over time. If you plan to use a condom, take two fresh ones from the package and put them in your pocket for that day only. Why two? If you tear one, you'll have a spare.

Another reason for condom failure is using the wrong lubricant. Never use any oil-based lubricant such hand lotion, baby oil, face cream, or petroleum jelly (Vaseline). The oil eats holes in the condom. Use water-based lubricants sold specifically for sexual use. One well-known brand is KY Jelly. It's available in virtually every drugstore and supermarket.

Don't buy lambskin condoms. They do not protect against sexually transmitted disease. Check the package to make sure you are buying latex condoms. If you are allergic to latex, choose condoms made from polyurethane or synthetic latex.

Open the package carefully, and make sure that you or your partner don't tear the condom. Never reuse a condom. They are made for one use only.

How Do I Put on a Condom?

Practice using a condom during masturbation. That way, you can avoid embarrassment or accidents when having sex with a partner.

1. Open the package carefully so you don't tear or rip the condom inside.
2. Do not unroll the condom before putting it on.
3. If not circumcised, pull the foreskin back.
4. Check that the reservoir tip is poking out from the middle of the roll, so you are sure the condom can be unrolled.

5. Hold the tip of the condom to squeeze out the air. This leaves some room at the end for the semen that comes out of the penis during ejaculation.
6. At this point, or earlier, you must be erect. You cannot put a condom on a soft penis.
7. Before any contact with your partner's mouth, anus, or genitals, place the condom on the glans and unroll onto the erect penis.
8. Unroll the condom down the penis until it covers its entire length.
9. After ejaculation and before your erection softens, hold the rim of the condom at the base of the penis.
10. Withdraw from contact with your partner.
11. Remove the condom from your penis.
12. Wrap it in paper or seal it in a plastic bag. Throw it in a covered trash can or bury it. Do not flush it down the toilet or litter the environment. (Condoms clog plumbing and few things are more disgusting than stepping on a used condom during a walk in the park.)

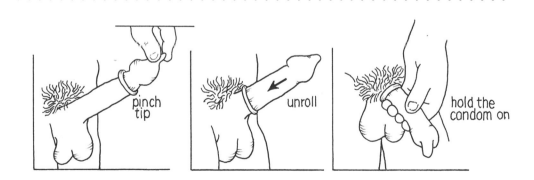

How to use the male condom

Should I Go to a Prostitute to "Learn How"?

No. Forget the stereotype of the good-hearted whore who will teach you the ropes. That person doesn't exist.

The real price of commercial sex is much greater than the fee you pay. Prostitution degrades both the seller and the buyer. The seller is too often a victim, controlled by a greedy and violent pimp and dependent on an abusive "boss" and dangerous "trade" for food, clothing, and shelter. Some 50 percent of street prostitutes in the U.S. are drug addicted. The numbers rise as high as 84 percent in some places, where addicts are driven to prostitution to support their crippling, lethal addiction.[12]

The buyer is degraded in turning the most intimate and powerful form of human communication into something cheap and shameful. The thrill doesn't last, and you may get more than you bargained for. One study in New York and Miami found that 30 percent of the women who traded sex for money or drugs were infected with the AIDS virus.[13] Among New York prostitutes, 26 percent had a history of gonorrhea, 18 percent had been infected with syphilis, and a significant number either didn't know or couldn't remember if they had ever had a sexually transmitted disease.[14]

What Women Want

·····

*In spite of what Thomas Jefferson wrote, all men
may be created equal, but not to all women.*

BILL COSBY

·····

*A*sk most women to pick their
handsome fantasy male, and
large numbers will exclaim, "John
DeSalvo!" Never heard of him?
Maybe, but you've surely seen his
handsome mug on a book rack
someplace. He's the leading cover
model for romance and science fic-
tion paperbacks. His face and form
grace such classic mind-benders (!) as
Savage Thunder and *Follow the
Moon.*

OK, so maybe you don't look
like John DeSalvo, but you may still
have a chance of getting a girlfriend.
Women choose their men for many
different reasons, and scientists (like
everybody else) wonder why women
pick as they do. When Australian sci-

Model John DeSalvo

entist Rob Brooks and California researcher John Endler took on that conundrum, they looked not at guys and gals, but guppies!

Among these fish, males do all the primping and preening, and females do all the choosing. The males are constantly displaying their color patterns in hopes of attracting a mate. Brooks observed the fishes' mating behavior to determine if all females define handsome in the same way.

Brooks and Endler found that, in general, the females preferred males with big tails and high-contrast color patterns. They usually found males with lots of orange and iridescent colors more appealing than their smaller-tailed, plainer competitors. But females varied in their choices. Some of the females rejected males with large areas of black coloration and an overall bright color pattern, while others accepted them eagerly.

Brooks says there's no "universal standard of sexual attractiveness"—and for good reason! He says differences in female choice help maintain genetic variability in a species. If different males and females mate, their offspring come out differently, and that's an advantage in the natural world. If some disease, predator, or catastrophe comes along, some of the variable individuals will survive, even if many others are killed. So the species continues, even if some of its members don't.

Women aren't fish, and their perception of "handsome" is more fine-tuned than a guppy's. Researchers in Japan used computers to "average" male faces. (That's done by mathematically combining the facial measurements of dozens of men.) The resulting composite is generally more pleasing to the human eye than any of the faces that went into building it. When ask to rate such faces, women surprised the researchers. They rejected the average male faces as—believe it or not—too masculine! During the fertile times in the menstrual cycle, when pregnancy is most likely to occur, women prefer a man's face that's 8 percent "feminized." At other times of the month, they choose an even more feminized face—from 15 to 20 percent.[15]

Other factors affect women's perceptions of sex appeal, too. Pat Barclay at McMaster University in Hamilton, Ontario, asked women to rate made-up dating service listings

2-FACE COMPOSITE

4-FACE COMPOSITE

An array of mathematically averaged faces

8-FACE COMPOSITE

16-FACE COMPOSITE

32-FACE COMPOSITE

One-on-One Dating Service

Name: Sam McDowell

Sex: Male

Date of Birth: June 30th, 1981

Education: 1st year University

Location: Hamilton

In Spare Time: Ultimate Frisbee, jogging, movies, swimming, travel

I'm looking for that someone special to share myself with. I'm caring, understanding, honest, and open-minded. I hope to meet someone who will be a good friend and good listener, who is straightforward and not just tell me things I want to hear. I don't need someone who looks like a movie star, but someone who takes relationships seriously, doesn't try to come across as something they are not, and who says what's on their mind but is willing to listen to other people's point of view. I do like to go out occasionally, but also enjoy time spent alone with that special someone. If you might be that person, I'd love to hear from you.

of eligible men. The listings contained identical photographs and identical write-ups, with one difference. In half of the cases, the list of hobbies and interests showed altruistic (generous, unselfish, helping and caring) activities such as volunteer refereeing or working with special needs children. The women rated the altruistic men as physically and sexually more attractive than the non-altruistic men. They also judged the altruistic men as better candidates for dates and for long-term relationships. Barclay thinks altruistic interests signal a man's good character. They raise his status as a potential life partner who will invest time in a relationship and in children.[16]

And women find a man like that sexy—even if he doesn't look like John DeSalvo.

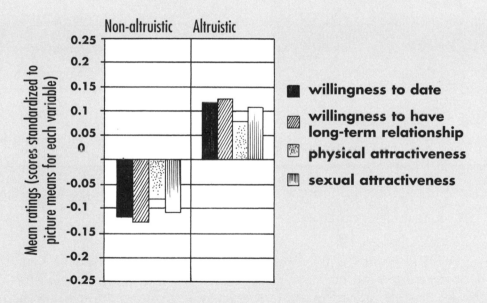

Is that face sexy? In one experiment, women answered "yes" if they thought the man was generous and caring.

CHAPTER THREE

QUESTIONS

YOUNG WOMEN ASK

There are three great questions which in life
we have over and over again to answer: Is it right or wrong?
Is it true or false? Is it beautiful or ugly?

• JOHN LUBBOCK •

Are Girls Growing Up Faster than They Used to?

No doubt about it. Between 1850 and 1950, the average age of menarche (first menstrual period) fell from 17 to 13.[1] Since then, the timing of menarche has changed only a little, but the first signs of puberty—including breast development and pubic hair—are showing up in younger and younger girls.

Puberty is now considered "precocious" (unusually early) for Caucasian girls at age 7 and African-American girls at age 6.[2] By age 8, nearly half of African-American girls and one in seven Caucasian girls have breast and/or pubic hair growth.[3] Experts guess that better nutrition may be the reason, but no one knows why for sure.

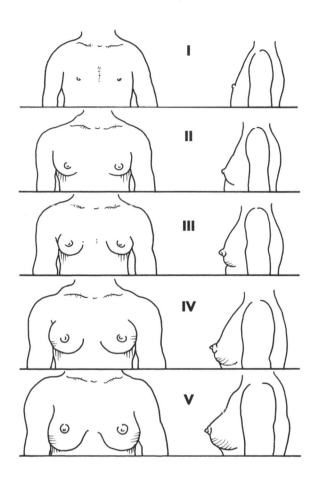

Female breast
development in stages
during adolescence

PUBERTAL EVENT[4]	AVERAGE AGE FOR CAUCASIAN GIRLS	AVERAGE AGE FOR AFRICAN-AMERICAN GIRLS
Breast development	9.96	8.87
Pubic hair	10.51	8.78
Menarche	12.88	12.16

My Boyfriend Says He'll Get "Blue Balls" if I Don't Have Sex With Him. What's He Talking About, and Is He Right?

If men stop sexual activity after a great deal of stimulation but before ejaculation, muscle tension in the lower abdomen may ease slowly. That causes an aching feeling some men call "blue balls." (Actually, women experience the feeling, too, but without the colorful name.) The ache goes away as muscles relax, and the extra blood that accumulated in the genitals moves out of the area. Time will do the job as well as an ejaculation. Female assistance is not needed.

How Can I Tell if My Boyfriend Is Circumcised or Uncircumcised?

It's easy to tell, just by looking. At birth, a sheath of skin called the foreskin, or prepuce, covers the head of the baby boy's penis. If the male is circumcised, the foreskin is surgically removed. The head is clearly visible even when the penis is flaccid (soft). Males who have not been circumcised still have a foreskin. It covers the head when the penis is soft and retracts during erection.

Worldwide, about one in four men are circumcised, but national customs vary. In Scandinavia, less than 2 percent of boys are circumcised.[5] In the United States, 60 percent are—making circumcision the most commonly performed operation in the nation.[6] In 1997, 1.2 million boys were circumcised. That's one every 26 seconds.[7]

The only medical reason for circumcision is a condition called preputial stenosis, in which a hardened skin grows at the tip of the foreskin. It occurs in less than 1 percent of baby boys.[8] Some circumcisions are done for religious reasons. Others are done under the mis-

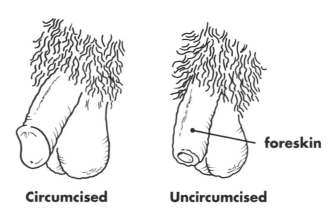

Circumcised　　**Uncircumcised**

foreskin

taken assumption that circumcision promotes genital cleanliness. Whether it's done or not makes no difference in male sexual performance or satisfaction. While most adult men don't mind having been circumcised, a few complain of feeling a lack of wholeness, thinking that their parents violated them, or pain during intercourse.

Do I Need an Intact Hymen to Be a Virgin?

The hymen is a thin membrane surrounding and partially covering the vaginal opening. It varies considerably in size and shape from one female to another. It may be absent at birth. Any object that enters the vagina—whether a finger, tampon, or penis—can stretch or break it. Many girls never know it's there and may never be aware of when it is broken. Some hurt and bleed when it is first disrupted. The hymen may open naturally as a girl grows, so its presence or absence reveals nothing about virginity.

Different types of hymens

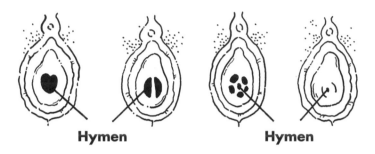

Hymen   **Hymen**

If I Have Only Oral or Anal Sex, Can I Say I'm Still a Virgin?

You can say anything you like, but you're missing the point. Intimate sexual contact takes many forms. If you are engaging in any of those forms, you are having sex. Since oral and anal sex are as risky as (or riskier than) penile-vaginal sex, clinging to the word "virgin" may let you fool yourself for a while, but don't expect the deception to protect you from the consequences of sexual activity.

Oral sex transfers diseases such as the human papillomavirus (HVP) just as readily as does vaginal intercourse. In fact, some studies suggest that the chance of contracting the AIDS virus through anal intercourse is even greater than through vaginal intercourse. The wall of the lower intestine is thin and easily injured, unlike the stronger, more elastic vaginal wall. The fragility of the colon membrane may explain, at least in part, the high rate of HIV transmission among men who have anal intercourse with men.

Why Am I Wet Between My Legs All the Time?

The Bartholin's glands, one on each side of the vaginal opening, secrete a thin, watery fluid. It prevents infections and keeps the vagina clean and healthy. Secretions from these glands increase naturally at puberty. The fluid is colorless and odorless. It should cause you no concern. If, however, you have secretions that sting or burn, look white or lumpy, or smell yeasty, see a doctor.

Vaginal secretions increase in quantity when a female becomes sexually excited. Along with fluids from the cervix, this natural lubricant eases the entry of the penis into the vagina during intercourse. A woman who is not sufficiently aroused may find she is too dry to accept her partner's penis comfortably.

What's an Orgasm, and How Can I Know if I've Had One?

An orgasm is a sudden release of muscular tension and blood accumulation in the genital area. The muscle group that supports the pelvic floor contacts rhythmically at 0.8-second intervals.[9] The contractions vary from a slight throbbing of the genitals in some people to large muscle movements and a flexing of the spine in others. Orgasm is brief, but the mind focuses on the brain waves it produces. If your body begins to move in ways you didn't intend, and waves of pleasure surge through you, you're probably having an orgasm.

I Don't Have Orgasms. Am I Normal?

Definitely. Only 29 percent of women report always having an orgasm with their partner (compared with 75 percent of men).[10] Many women experience orgasm only when the clitoris is stimulated by touch. Some never do. In one survey, two thirds of women said they did not consider orgasm important to their sexual well-being.[11]

"Sexual response in females is more complicated than in males," writes physician Mark Levie. While men recognize an erection as an obvious physical sign of arousal, women's responses are more subjective. "A woman may not recognize her [sexual] sensations: throbbing, tingling, warmth, engorgement [filling with blood]," Levie says. Feelings of emotional closeness, bonding, commitment, love, affection, and acceptance may be more important.[12]

I Have No Interest in Sex. Should I See a Doctor?

Doctors consider a woman "sexually dysfunctional" only if something about her sexuality causes her "personal distress." Some women feel anxious because they don't want sex, seldom or never feel aroused, or don't have orgasms. Other women may experience the same things but not be bothered by them. If your sexuality worries you, a physical exam and a visit to a counselor are a good idea.

Some women avoid sex because it's uncomfortable. Their vaginas stay too dry for the penis to enter comfortably. A low level of the hormone estrogen may cause this condition. Too little estrogen causes the vagina to grow smooth, thin, and pale. Its fluid secretion may fall by half or more. The vaginal environment becomes more alkaline (with a pH greater than 5). The change in acidity disrupts the normal populations of bacteria that live in the vagina, and the risk of infection increases. Too little estrogen may also cause problems with the urethra and bladder, bringing on frequent urination or difficulty controlling the urine flow. Vaginal dryness comes from many sources, including breast-feeding, cancer treatments, certain drugs, ovariectomy (removal of the ovaries), cigarette smoking, chemical sensitivities to soaps or perfumes, even tight-fitting clothing. Estrogen pills or patches help some women. Over-the-counter lubricants sold in drugstores relieve the dryness that interferes with intercourse.

Two other medical conditions may disrupt female sexual functioning. Fortunately, both can be treated. The first is vaginismus. It is an involuntary tightening of the muscles around the lower part of the vagina. The muscles contract so strongly that penetration is impossible. The condition causes physical pain as well as distress, when a woman wants to have intercourse but cannot. Vaginismus may also interfere with medical examinations. The cause may be fear arising from sexual abuse, anger in a relationship, anxiety about pregnancy, a belief that the vagina is too small, and many others. A course of treatment involving relaxation exercises along with behavior training nearly always overcomes vaginismus.[13]

The second treatable condition is dyspareunia. It is pain associated with sexual intercourse. It may be pain of the vulva or vagina, or deeper abdominal pain felt during thrusting of the penis. It's important to treat the condition early before it leads to difficulty in a loving relationship. Treatment of the physical condition that produces the pain, along with relaxation exercises and counseling, are effective for many women.

What Are PMS and PMDD, and Do I Have Them?

In the days before the menstrual flow begins, some girls and women feel irritable, tense, and sad. They may complain of bloating, food cravings, and tenderness of the breasts.

These symptoms are usually mild and disappear when the menstrual flow begins.

If symptoms are severe, they may earn the labels PMS (premenstrual syndrome) or PMDD (premenstrual dysphoric disorder). One drug manufacturer attributes PMDD to an imbalance of the neurotransmitter serotonin in the brain, but hard evidence is scant. Nevertheless, drugs that prevent the serotonin from being reabsorbed into the nerve cells that released it are considered "frontline" therapy for PMDD. These are the same drugs often prescribed to treat depression and anxiety.

For most women, eating right, exercising, and managing the stress in their lives is enough to keeps premenstrual symptoms under control. Dietary supplements, including calcium or vitamin B-6, help some. Exercise is thought to raise levels of natural pain relievers called beta-endorphins in the blood and brain.

While severe cramps, very heavy flows, or deep depression can benefit from medical treatment, it pays to be skeptical about the PMS and PMDD labels. "I have concerns about . . . blaming women's behavior and bad moods on women's reproductive function," says Nadia Stotland, a specialist in psychiatry and women's medicine at Rush Medical College in Chicago.[14] Both male and female hormones affect behavior and mood, she says. Singling out women at a particular time in their cycle for a disease label may do little good for women or for medicine.

The Food and Drug Administration advises that "drugs should be used only to treat women whose symptoms are severe enough to interfere with functioning at work or school, or with social activities and relationships."[15] The long-term risks of such drugs are not known, and the potential for harm is real.

Each breast is a mammary gland. It produces milk to feed an infant. On the chest, you can see the nipple from which milk flows when nursing a baby. Around that is an area of darkened bumpy skin called the areola. The areola contains glands that secrete sebum, an oily lubricant that keeps the nipple supple.

Under the skin lie 15 to 20 lobes, each containing many smaller segments called lobules. The lobules produce milk and empty it into the milk ducts, which carry milk to the nipple. Connective tissue—called Cooper's ligaments—supports the lobes, lobules, and ducts, while fat cushions them. In the teen and young adult years, about 80 to 85 percent of a woman's breast tissue is fat.[16] Beneath the breast lies the big muscle of the chest, the pectoralis major.

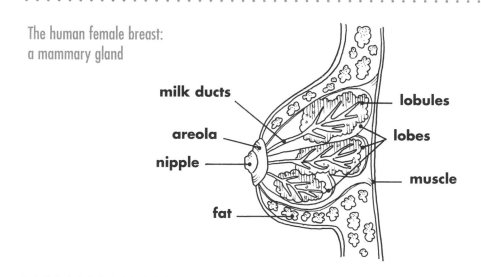

The human female breast: a mammary gland

milk ducts

areola

nipple

fat

lobules

lobes

muscle

Breasts grow during puberty under the influence of the female hormone estrogen. They will not grow as a result of any cream, pill, vitamin preparation, or herbal supplement you may see advertised in magazines or on TV. Save yourself a lot of money and a lot of worry by accepting and appreciating the beautiful breasts you have.

I Have Breast Pain. Is That Normal?

Doctors call breast pain mastalgia. It often occurs on certain days of the menstrual cycle, usually just before the flow begins. Commonly, both breasts feel tender, swollen, or sore. The breasts may throb or burn, or you may occasionally feel a sharp pain. Pain that is not associated with the menstrual cycle tends to come and go. It may happen in one or both breasts and extend into the armpit or down the arm.

Mastalgia is common and rarely serious, but if your breasts hurt, it's a good idea to check with your doctor to rule out any serious problem. Treatment when needed may include supportive bras, vitamin E supplements, pain-relieving drugs, or hormone therapy.

Are Breast Implants Safe?

You decide.

In 1999 the Institute of Medicine (of the National Academy of Sciences) reported that local complications with silicone breast implants were their major safety issue. These include swelling, inflammation, bleeding, infection, and poor healing. Other risks include:

- *contraction of the capsule.* Scar tissue, called a capsule, forms around a breast implant. If it tightens too much, it can cause the

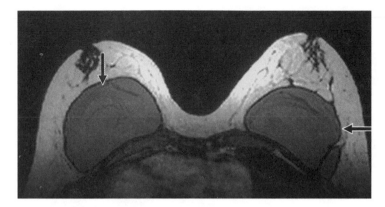

An MRI (magnetic resonance image) shows rupture in both breast implants.

breast to be hard, lumpy, and painful. Contracture can be corrected with additional surgery, but it can also then happen again.

- *deflation or rupture.* If the bag that contains the implant material breaks, the filler leaks out. Leakage can cause hard knots, tingling, swelling, numbness, burning, decreased breast size, and other symptoms. Rupture may also occur without symptoms. The implant material may migrate, forming lumps in the chest, abdomen, or arm.
- *hematoma or seroma.* Blood or blood plasma can collect inside the breast cavity.
- *extrusion.* Unstable, weakened, or dead tissue may allow the breast implant to push out through the skin.
- *inability to breast-feed.* Two thirds of women who have implants are never able to breast-feed a child.[17]
- *dissatisfaction with the results.* Complaints typically include wrinkling, uneven size, implant shifting, undesired shape, visible scars, sloshing (of saline implants), and a hard, unnatural, or uncomfortable feel. Unexpected milk production or leakage occurs in some cases. Nipples and breasts may become more or less sensitive to touch than before surgery. Calcium deposits around implants may give a marbled, lumpy feel.

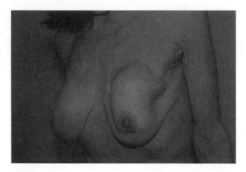

Before

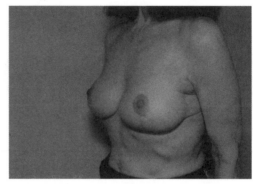

After

Leaking gel implants were removed and, upon the advice of her surgeon, this woman underwent a breast lift to reshape her own breast tissue, instead of having new saline filled implants.

The National Cancer Institute says that no evidence links implants to breast cancer. However, because implants interfere with mammography (the X-ray procedure used to find breast cancers), tumors are found later in women who have implants than in those who don't. That increases the risk of death from breast cancer, because lifesaving treatment is delayed.

Despite these facts, our cultural love affair with breast implants shows no sign of abating. About two million American women have silicone breast implants. In 2000 more than 200,000 women had the surgery to increase their breast size. The numbers who chose implants for reasons of appearance (as compared with reconstructive surgery after breast cancer) doubled between 1997 and 2000.[18]

Should I Have Breast Reduction?

Breast reduction can be done for reasons of appearance. More often, however, it is prompted by medical concerns. Breast reduction may be achieved by a surgical procedure called reduction mammoplasty or by liposuction, in which fat is withdrawn from the breast with a vacuuming instrument.

Breast reduction decreases back, neck, and shoulder pain arising from supporting the weight of large breasts. It can also relieve breast pain and numbness in the fingers and hands. It can prevent rashes under the breasts and deep grooves that form in the shoulders from the pressure of bra straps. But be warned that breast reduction is not risk free. In some patients, breast tissues harden and collect deposits of calcium. Also, reduction may make later breast-feeding difficult or impossible.

What Is the G-spot, and Do I Have One?

The G-spot is said to be an area inside the wall of the vagina that is especially sensitive to sexual stimulation. It was named for Ernest Grafenberg, who published a paper about it in the *International Journal of Sexology* in 1950. In his article, Dr. Grafenberg told some stories he had heard from his female patients, but he presented no clinical or anatomical proof.

"The scientific evidence that is usually cited to support the existence of a G-spot is so inadequate as to be almost laughable," says Terrence Hines of Pace University. If the G-spot existed, Hines believes, it would have many neurons (nerve cells) that would send impulses to the brain. No such structure has been found, he says, although some women do occasionally report experiencing pleasurable sensations in part of the front wall of the vagina—starting near the clitoris and ending near the bladder.

"Some women might feel very bad about themselves and their sexuality if they can't find the G-spot—but there is nothing there to find," Dr. Hines says.[19]

What Is a Douche, and Should I Use One?

A douche is a "cleaning solution" pumped into the vagina. Many different types are available in drugstores, but you should never use one unless a doctor tells you to.

When normal and healthy, the interior of the vagina is a highly acid environment (pH 3.5 to 4.5). The major reason for the acidity is that vaginal bacteria change sugar from the blood into lactic acid. The acid environment retards the growth of harmful microbes and prevents infections. Douching changes the pH and kills beneficial bacteria. That gives the abnormal ones a chance to thrive. In one research study, douching tripled the risk of a bacterial infection of the vagina.[20]

No matter what you've heard, douching does not prevent pregnancy. In fact, some studies show that it increases pregnancy risks by propelling sperm into the uterus. Leave the "cleaning" of the vagina to nature.

Can I Get an Infection of My Vulva or Vagina Even if I'm Not Having Sex?

Irritation of the vagina or vulva can result from many causes. Contact dermatitis, or irritation of the skin, can arise from an allergic response to soaps, deodorants, underwear, detergents, spermicides, cleansing wipes, sexual lubricants, sanitary pads, or medicines such as hemorrhoid preparations. In rare cases, a woman may be allergic to her partner's sperm.

Vaginal infections happen in females, whether they are having sex or not. Such conditions are so common that ten million American women visit the doctor annually for treatment of vaginitis.[21] If you are among them, chances are you have one of three common complaints.

The most frequent is a yeast infection, or candidiasis. Infection with *Candida* or *Torulopsis* species (or other kinds of yeasts) affects three out of four women at some time in their lives. About 40 to 45 percent have more than one yeast infection.[22] Symptoms may include a curdy, white, yeasty-smelling discharge and burning, itching, or soreness of the vulva. As many as 15 to 20 percent of vaginal yeast infections have no symptoms.[23]

Another kind of vaginitis is bacterial vaginosis, or BV. Bacteria called anaerobes, meaning "without oxygen," normally live in the vagina. So do the "friendly" bacteria *Lactobacillus*. They produce hydrogen peroxide, a natural microbe-killing chemical. When the anaerobes overrun the *Lactobacilli* in numbers, the chemistry of the healthy vagina is disrupted. The first symptom of BV may be an unusual discharge. It may be clear or colored, thin or thick, or fishy smelling.

The third type is trichomoniasis, caused by the microscopic one-celled organism *Trichomonas vaginalis*. *Trichomonas* infects the vagina and often the urinary tract as well. The infection may produce no symptoms, or it may cause a smelly yellow-green discharge. It is often accompanied by discomfort in the vulva or pain and burning during urination.

Although yeast infections, bacterial vaginosis, and trichomoniasis can show up in women who aren't having sex, they can also be transmitted sexually, so sex partners must be treated at the same time as the patient.

Trichomonas vaginalis, an organism that infects the vagina. Notice the four flagella it uses to propel itself.

Girls and women who experience any unusual discharge, burning, itching, or discomfort in the genital area should see a doctor immediately. Untreated BV can infect the uterus and Fallopian tubes. Trichomoniasis increases the risk of infection with HIV, the virus that causes AIDS. If you are diagnosed with a vaginal infection, your health care provider may prescribe pills for you to take by mouth, or a cream, gel, or capsule to put in your vagina. It's important to use the medicine exactly as your doctor tells you.

What Can I Expect When I Get My First Pelvic Exam?

When you go in for your checkup, you'll first receive all the usual health checks. The doctor or nurse will ask your medical history, take your blood pressure, listen to your heart, and check your reflexes. He or she will measure your height and weight and take samples of blood and urine for testing.

For the pelvic (genital and reproductive organs) part of the exam, your health care provider will ask you to lie on your back. You will place your feet in stirrups at the end of the table. Your body will be covered with a sheet, so you need not feel naked or embarrassed. Your breasts will be felt for lumps and examined for discharges. Your armpits will be checked for swollen lymph nodes. This exam detects breast cancers. (Ask your doctor to show you how to examine your own breasts.)

The doctor or nurse practitioner will look at your vulva and check for any signs of disease. Your health care provider will also put a finger in your vagina and press down on your abdomen with his or her other hand to find your uterus and ovaries. From the feel of these organs, the doctor can tell a lot about whether they are functioning normally.

Every year or two (your doctor will tell you when), you'll need a Pap smear. This test checks for abnormal, possibly cancerous cells in the cervix. The cervix is the part of the uterus closest to the vagina. Never miss a Pap test! It's a real lifesaver. Since the 1960s, the death rate from cervical cancer has fallen by 70 to 80 percent, largely because of the early diagnosis the Pap smear provides.[24]

To perform the test, your health care provider will insert a device called a speculum into your vagina. It opens the vagina, making the cervix easy to see. It doesn't hurt, but the speculum may be cold, and

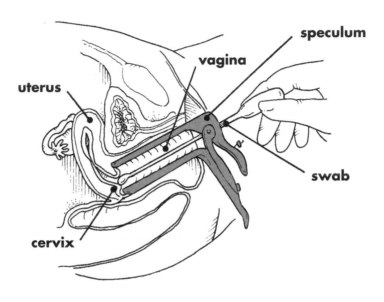

speculum

vagina

uterus

swab

cervix

Getting cells from the cervix for a Pap smear

you may feel pressure. With the speculum in place, the doctor uses a wooden spatula, brush, or cotton swab to take some cells from the cervix. You may feel slight discomfort as the sample is taken. The cells are then placed on a glass microscope slide. The slide goes to a laboratory, where a specialist examines the cells under a microscope. Depending on where you live, you should get your results back in a week or two. Chances are, your test will come back normal. If the cells look suspicious or if the test material was inadequate in some way, your doctor may ask you to repeat the test.

If you feel anxious about the pelvic exam, try to breathe deeply and relax. Listening to music, daydreaming, or carrying on a conversation with the doctors and nurses may keep your mind off the procedure. If you want to know what's happening, ask your doctor to show you the speculum and explain step-by-step what the examination involves. Most of all, try not to worry. The exam is quick, nearly painless, and extremely important to your health and well-being. If you are having sex, try to arrange for your partner to visit the doctor with you. The doctor can discuss with you both how to prevent unwanted pregnancies and disease.

You should see a qualified heath care provider for a routine exam as soon as you become sexually active, but no later than age 18. If you don't want to see a physician in private practice, clinics are available in most communities. Ask your school counselor, contact your local health department, or Planned Parenthood at 1-800-230-PLAN.

Should I Use a Female Condom?

Yes, the female condom offers good protection against both pregnancy and sexually transmitted diseases. The closed inner ring of the female condom covers the cervix and is anchored behind the pubic bone. The other ring, which is open, rests outside the vagina and covers the vulva. Here's how to use one:

1. Find the inner ring of the condom and hold it between your thumb and middle finger.
2. Squeeze the ring together and insert as far as possible into the vagina, making sure that the inner ring is past the pubic bone.
3. The outer ring should be outside the vagina.
4. Make sure the condom has not become twisted. (These steps can be done as much as eight hours ahead of time.)
5. Lubricate the penis with water-based lubricant. (Do not use Vaseline, body lotion, or any oil-based lubricant.)

6. When your partner's penis enters you, hold the plastic sheath to cover your labia. (This is important to preventing both pregnancy and sexually transmitted diseases.)

7. After intercourse, while standing, squeeze and twist the outer ring to make sure the semen stays inside. Remove the condom by pulling gently.

8. Use only once. Do not flush. Wrap in paper or a plastic bag, and throw in a covered garbage can.

The female condom has some advantages over the more familiar male version. It allows girls and women to have greater control over sexual situations. Female condoms are made of polyurethane. They are

How to use a female condom

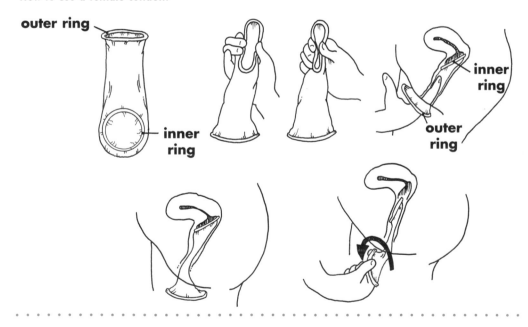

stronger and store longer than male condoms. Because the female condom can be inserted up to eight hours before intercourse, it doesn't "spoil the mood."

It takes practice to learn to insert the female condom properly. Practice in private until you become comfortable with the procedure. Also, you must learn to hold the condom in place during penetration, so that the penis thrusts inside the condom, not between the condom and the vaginal wall. Don't try to use a male condom and a female condom at the same time.

Should I Use a Spermicide With a Condom?

Yes. Spermicides are chemicals that kill sperm without upsetting the chemistry of the female vagina. Some condoms come already lubricated with a spermicide, but the amount is too little to do much good. It's best to increase your protection against pregnancy by using an additional spermicidal suppository, foam, film, or gel with the condom. One study found a first-year pregnancy rate of condom with spermicide of only 3 percent.25 Forget what you've heard about spermicides preventing sexually transmitted diseases. They don't. In fact, they may actually increase the risk of infection with the AIDS virus.

Are Women "Turned On" by Sexy Pictures Like Men Are?

Some say they aren't. They object to such material as pornographic. Others, apparently, find erotic images sexually stimulating—even if they aren't aware of it. Scientists at the University of Washington studied women while they looked at erotic videos. They placed volunteers with their hips inside a magnetic resonance imaging (MRI) unit. They measured blood flow to the genitals and enlargement of the clitoris in their volunteers. The MRI pictures showed that the clitoris can expand as much as 85 percent and blood flow can increase by as much as 40 percent in response to pictures alone.

"I think the most astonishing thing about this study," says researcher Julie Heiman, "is that women can get aroused under these circumstances. It shows how robust the sexual response really is."[26]

Most women probably won't be impressed by Heiman's findings. Edward Laumann at the University of Chicago found that only 11 percent of women watch X-rated movies or videos, only 4 percent read sexually explicit books or magazines, and only 4 percent enjoy watching nude male dancers. Unlike men, women never call phone-in sex services.[27]

What Is Female Circumcision?

Female circumcision is misnamed. It is in no way similar to male circumcision. It is better described as female genital mutilation. It is performed to preserve virginity until marriage and to reduce a woman's sexual pleasure so she will not be tempted to be unfaithful to her husband.

The mutilation can vary from removal of a small part of the clitoris to removal of the entire labia and clitoris. It is most often done without anesthetic and without clean surgical instruments. Once the female genitalia are cut away, the site is sewn tightly closed, leaving only a small opening for elimination of urine. Complications include infections, bleeding, pain, and death. After healing, risks are high for pain during intercourse, urinary infections and blockages, and difficulties in childbirth.

The World Health Organization estimates that some two million girls between the ages of four and ten undergo the procedure annually.[28] The total number who have survived such mutilation worldwide is estimated at 138 million.[29] More than 80 percent of females in Egypt, Sudan, Ethiopia, and Somalia have been mutilated in this way. Numbers are thought to run at 50 percent or more in Mali, Nigeria, Chad, and several other African countries.[30] Although illegal, the practice continues among certain immigrant groups in the United States.

Who Knows What the Nose Knows?

·····

Science increases our power . . . as it lowers our pride.
HERBERT SPENCER

·····

The sea slug, *Aplysia.*

Now there's an expert on sex.

Equipped with both male and female sex organs, this shell-less subtidal mollusk lives alone most of the year. It loses its self-sufficiency, however, when the mating season comes around. In summer, sea slugs congregate in breeding colonies called (yes, it's true!) brothels. They crawl around over one another, trading sperm. A slug's penis is long enough to reach its own female sperm-storage organs, but slugs never make babies that way. Even among these dual-sexed creatures, it takes two to become parents.

The marvel of sea slug sex lies in how these virtually blind loners find each other for a few days annually. Their call to the brothel is neither sight nor sound, but a chemical compound called attractin. Released into water from egg-laying glands, attractin makes sea slugs irresistible to other sea slugs. Attractin is a pheromone. Pheromones are communication chemicals. They are released by one individual. They affect the behavior or body functions of another.

All animals produce a "cocktail of chemicals" that influence attraction, mating, or both, says researcher Sherry Painter of the University of Texas Medical Branch at Galveston. "A lot of people don't like to think about it," Painter says, "but humans use pheromones too."

Some of those human uses have been known for years. In 1986 researchers in Philadelphia collected sweat from men's underarms and dabbed it on the upper lips of women. The women reported smelling nothing but the alcohol that had been used to extract the "eau de sweat." After three months of this dabbing, however, those women who had experienced formerly irregular menstrual cycles became as predictable as the tides. The investigators concluded that some chemical released from the male body could control the timing of the female menstrual cycle.

In some cases, we are aware of an odor's sexual appeal. Participants in one research project were asked whether they found certain smells sexually stimulating. The proportion answering "yes" was:

Body odor without perfume	48%
Body odor with perfume	46%
Genital odor	32%
Odor after sexual intercourse	28%
Underarm odor	23%
Breast odor	21%
Breath	16%[31]

Scientist Sherry Painter and her subject, the sea slug.

"When you meet someone new whom you find attractive, you probably 'like the smell of him,' and this helps predispose you to romance," writes Helen Fisher in *Anatomy of Love*.[32] For women, that odor may have more to do with reproduction than romance. A research team at the University of Chicago had women sniff men's two-night-old T-shirts. The women preferred the smells of men whose genes most closely resembled their father's genes, but not their own.[33] In similar experiments, British scientists found that women chose smells associated with genes that encode immune system functions complementary to their own. Researchers think that choosing a mate with the disease-fighting genes a woman lacks makes for stronger, healthier offspring.[34]

Other scientists say that it's not what you smell, but what you don't, that matters. Odorless chemicals may send their messages to the brain through a little-understood structure called the vomeronasal organ (VNO). The organ is a series of tiny ducts in the wall dividing the nostrils. The VNO is so small that its existence in humans was long questioned. But in 1991 it was found and mapped.

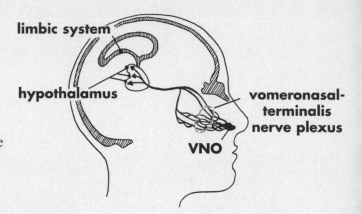

The vomeronasal organ in nose

Evidence is mounting that the tiny VNO may be active in humans. Researchers at Rockefeller and Yale Universities think they have found a gene that controls detection of one human pheromone. The gene contains codes for a receptor that may bind to the pheromone when it enters the nose. Locking onto the receptor could trigger nerve impulses that travel from the VNO to the limbic system of the brain. That's where the strongest and most basic of human emotions arise. Emotions like love.

If you're skeptical, go ask a sea slug.

CHAPTER FOUR

QUESTIONS
COUPLES ASK

When you loved me and I loved you
Then both of us were born anew.

• WILLIAM CARTWRIGHT, 1636 •

Do Males and Females Think Differently About Sex?

It appears they do. UCLA researchers Letitia Peplau and Linda Garnets say, "Women romanticize. . . . Men sexualize."[1] Women have a "relational or partner-centered" attitude toward sex. Men have a "body-centered or recreational" approach.[2] The same differences are found in both homosexual and heterosexual males and females.[3]

Women say they want intimacy from sexual encounters. They view sex as an expression of affection toward another person.[4] When women fantasize, they imagine a familiar partner in the context of affection and commitment.

Men say they want sexual variety. They believe that physical gratification is the goal of sex. Men fantasize about specific sex acts or sex organs or about sex with strangers or multiple partners.[5]

In national surveys, teen girls say they have sex because they are in love or hope to marry their partner. Teen boys say they want the physical sensation of sex, and they'll get it whenever they get a chance.[6] Males are more likely than females to feel that their friends expect them to have sex, or that their partners expect sex as part of a relationship. Boys say they feel they must have intercourse by a certain age to prove their manhood. Girls rarely report such an expectation for considering themselves women.

In addition, men think about sex more than women do. In a U.S. survey, 54 percent of men said they think about sex at least once a day. Only 19 percent of women reported doing so.[7] According to the Kinsey Institute, males ages 12 to 19 think about sex every five minutes.[8] If that's true, the average teenage male has nearly 200 sexual thoughts daily during his waking hours.

What's Sex Appeal?

Looking for sex appeal is like shopping for wallpaper. You don't know what you're after, but you know what you want when you see it. Sex appeal is that indescribable something that draws your attention from across the room. You can't say why, but that person is attractive. Your heart starts to pump and your palms get sweaty . . . but why? Scientists who try to define and measure sex appeal have come up with only two reliable predictors. The first is facial symmetry. A symmetrical face is the same on the left side as on the right. Some people have more symmetrical faces than others do. In general, both men and women find a symmetrical face appealing.

The second variable is body shape—specifically, the ratio of waist to hip measurement. Women like a 0.9 ratio in their men.[9] Men are

Reese Witherspoon   Ben Affleck

Here are two actors with very symmetrical faces. However, cover half of one image with a piece of paper. Then look at the face with the other half covered. Perfect symmetry is rare.

attracted to women with a waist-to-hip ratio between 0.6 and 0.7. This is the female "hourglass" shape, and men say it's sexy, regardless of the woman's weight, height, or body build.[10] Scientists think reproductive fitness is the reason why. When estrogen levels are right for childbearing, a woman deposits fat around her hips, making her waist smaller by comparison. Men unconsciously conclude that a woman with this ratio is probably young enough and strong enough to survive pregnancy and deliver a healthy child. Her "sex appeal" has been imprinted on the male brain throughout evolutionary history, biologists say. But why women prefer a 0.9 ratio in their men remains unexplained.

Models Kate Moss and Emme are two
different sizes but they both have that
appealing waist-to-hip ratio.

What happens when body size and face symmetry conflict? It's the eyes, not the thighs, that matter. When presented with different combinations of faces and forms, attractive features won male approval, regardless of body shape.[11]

Why Do People Have Sex?

Writes Wardell Pomeroy in his book *Boys and Sex*:

Sex in all its forms is a normal natural part of being human. What happens in the course of a sexual act is a pleasure beyond any of the other responses we make to the world we live in, and aside from its function of creating new life, it is a universal enjoyment, found in every society everywhere in the world.[12]

The road to this "universal enjoyment" is not smooth. Thirty percent of people never again have sex with the person they lose their virginity to. Three in four females report that they do not enjoy their first intercourse. Fewer than one in ten achieves orgasm during first intercourse.[13]

"Remember, penises and vaginas can't love each other," Pomeroy writes. "Only people can do that."[14]

Why Do Some Couples Choose Not to Have Sex?

In one study, the top three reasons were fear of pregnancy, a firm decision to wait, and concern about AIDS and other sexually transmitted diseases. The graph on the following page shows more.[15]

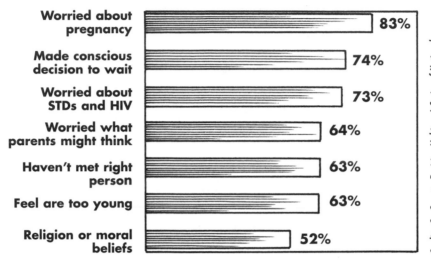

TO HAVE SEX ... OR NOT?

Worried about pregnancy	83%
Made conscious decision to wait	74%
Worried about STDs and HIV	73%
Worried what parents might think	64%
Haven't met right person	63%
Feel are too young	63%
Religion or moral beliefs	52%

Credit: SexSmarts: Decision Making: A Series of National Surveys of Teens About Sex. Kaiser Family Foundation and Seventeen Magazine, September 2000

What Kinds of Sex Are Young Adults Having, with Whom, and How Often?

For the majority, the answer is none. Most teens either have never had sex or have been sexually inactive for the past three months, a finding that implies that the majority of teens are not regularly sexually active.

Among those who are sexually active, patterns of activity vary. For example:

- More boys (12.2 percent) than girls (4.4 percent) begin having sex before they are 13.[16]

- Although penile-vaginal sex between male and female is the most common form of sexual intimacy between ages 13 and 19, one study conducted at a metropolitan clinic found that 15 percent of the sexually active young women and 22 percent of the young men had engaged in anal sex at some time.[17]

- In 1999, 16 percent of the sexually experienced high school students (19 percent of males and 13 percent of females) reported sexual intercourse with four or more partners at some time in their lives. That number was *down* 3 percent from 1993.[18]

- Teens who stay in school are less likely to be having sex than those who drop out of school.[19]

- Most girls have their first sexual intercourse with someone close to them in age. First sexual partners range from a year or two younger to a year or two older for about 60 percent.[20]

- On the average, sexually active teenagers tend to have intercourse two to three times per month, with males having sex more often than females.[21]

- The average sexually experienced, unmarried adolescent has sex during eight months of the year, and one quarter have sex during fewer than six months of the year.[22] The most likely months are April and August. The most common days, Friday and Saturday.[23]

- In a 1996 study of high school students in Los Angeles County, 35 percent of those students who said they were virgins reported masturbating with a partner (21 percent) or having oral sex (14 percent).[24]

- In a 1990 national survey of sexually experienced teens ages 12 to 17, over half were sure or almost sure they would have sex within the next year, though only one quarter "really wanted to."[25]

Should We Have Sexual Intercourse if We Are in Love?

Consider the nature of love first. Then we'll turn to the question of intercourse.

The feelings we call love come from surges of hormones in the blood and from neurotransmitters in the brain. The physical effects of those chemical changes range from a sinking feeling in the stomach to flushed cheeks, sweaty palms, loss of appetite, and the inability to think about anything except the loved one.

Researchers in London worked with volunteers who said they were "truly and madly" in love. The scientists used MRI (magnetic resonance imaging) machines to take pictures of the "loving" brain at work. When the lovers looked at photographs of their loved ones, four distinct brain regions showed increased blood flow and energy-burning activity. These regions lie in the brain's emotion-processing centers

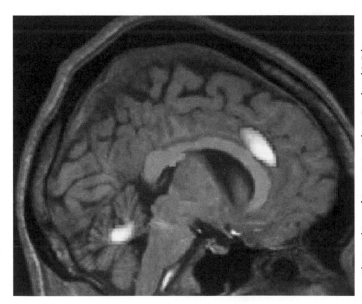

An MRI showing the brain's response to feelings of love.

From "The Neural Basis of Romantic Love" by A. Bartels and S. Zeki, published in *NeuroReport*, 11(17): 3829–3834.

where feelings of contentment and excitement are generated. Active in these areas is the neurotransmitter dopamine, known to induce a happy state of mind. One of the active regions is associated with sensations in the stomach, which might account for the "butterfly" feeling experienced by people in love. While some areas in the brain went into overdrive at the sight of the loved one, others dropped into neutral. Least active were the brain areas that handle negative emotions such as depression, anxiety, and aggression.[26]

Watching changes in body chemistry and behavior, scientists have identified three distinct stages of romantic love: lust, infatuation, and attachment. Lust is love at first sight or an immediate sexual attraction. The hormone testosterone produces a strong initial interest in a possible mate. Both males and females have testosterone. Males make testosterone in their testicles and adrenal glands. Females make it in smaller quantities, in their adrenal glands.

Infatuation is the second stage. It's the feeling of being "in love." "When you are infatuated," says Rutgers anthropologist Helen Fisher, "various chemicals, including [the neurotransmitter] dopamine, are released in your brain that work very much like amphetamines. . . . Lovers have all that energy—they can stay awake all night without feeling the least bit tired the next day, they lose weight, they feel optimistic, giddy, and full of life. They're high on natural speed."[27]

The "in love" phase generally lasts between 18 months and three years. During that time, levels of another neurotransmitter, norepinephrine, remain elevated. Lovers get "high" on a cocktail of their own brain chemicals. After a while, however, the neurotransmitter levels begin to drop, or nerve endings in the brain lessen their response to them. Then it's either break-up time—when the couple ends their relationship and moves on to seek a fresh neurotransmitter "fix"—or they make a long-term commitment.

Lasting love or attachment develops after infatuation fades. The thrill of being "in love" disappears, to be replaced by "loving." These are warm, secure feelings of safety and contentment experienced by those lucky (and wise) in the ways of love. Attachment depends partly on the hormone oxytocin produced in the hypothalamus. That same hormone floods the bloodstream of a new mother. It prompts her to fall madly in love with her baby. But men make it, too, if in smaller quantities. In both sexes, it strengthens emotional responses and makes memories of the loved one easier to retrieve while apart.

Long-term relationships boost levels of brain chemicals called endorphins. Endorphins are the body's natural painkillers. They produce feelings of security and well-being. Although proof is lacking, some scientists speculate that time spent with those we love boosts endorphin levels. When separated, endorphin levels fall, and we find ourselves missing loved ones.

Falling in love can be a thrilling, if frightening, experience. Infatuated lovers idealize one another, overlooking each other's weakness and seeing only the strengths. As time goes on, however, the gleam of adoration dims. Hormonal levels wane, neurotransmitters diminish, and that perfect prince or princess doesn't look so perfect anymore. For this reason, loving relationships in youth tend to be frequent, brief, and sometimes stormy. The stakes get higher if sex is involved, because the intimacy of sex compounds the risk of emotional hurt. The end of the infatuation stage hurts for couples who postponed sex. It can be devastating for those who didn't.

So deciding whether to inject sex into a youthful romance is more complicated than it may seem. You can't trust that feeling of, "I'll love this perfect person forever." Chances are, you won't. Don't let a boyfriend or girlfriend blackmail you into sex either. "If you loved me, you would have sex with me," is absurd. True love is unconditional. It accepts and values a loved one for himself or herself. It places no demands on sexual performance. It respects the right of the loved one to say no without having to defend or justify the decision.

If We Have Intercourse Now, Will We Regret It Later?

Chances are, you will. In one survey, more than half of males and nearly three quarters of females said they wished they had waited until they were older.[28]

How Can We Know if We Are Ready to Have Sex?

That's hard to say, but there's a good way to know if you are *not* ready. If you feel too shy, too embarrassed, or too "romantic" to discuss pregnancy and sexually transmitted diseases with your partner, then you are not ready for sex. Your relationship is not strong enough, and your communication is not good enough to make a sexual relationship work. People who are ready for sex plan for the good health and future happiness of themselves *and* their partners.

There's another good self-check: If you worry that your mother, father, guardian, best friend, minister, employer, or favorite teacher might find out you are having sex, then you're not ready. Couples who marry or live together let the world know that they are sexual partners. They don't fear disapproval, embarrassment, or rejection. If you're not ready for people to know what you are doing, then you're not ready to do it.

Must Both Partners Have an Orgasm at the Same Time for Sex to be Good?

No. In fact, simultaneous orgasms are rare. They happen mostly in romance novels and "R" movies. Forget what you've read about all-night lovemaking, too. Studies at two German universities found that levels of the hormone prolactin rise sharply after orgasm. "The prolactin surge may signal the brain and reproductive organs that 'once is enough,'" says scientist Michael Exton.[29]

What's the Risk of an Unwanted Pregnancy?

Among high school students in the United States, about one in every seven girls has been pregnant and 1 in every 14 boys has made someone pregnant before graduation rolls around.[30] More than four out of every ten teen girls will get pregnant at least once before age 20. That's about 900,000 teen pregnancies annually in the United States.[31] Among teens 15 to 19 years old, nearly eight out of every ten pregnancies are unplanned and unwanted.[32]

Young adults in the United States got smarter about sex and contraception in the 1990s. Between 1991 and 1997, the teen pregnancy rate dropped by 2.3 percent.[33] Between 1998 and 2000, the teen birthrate dropped 3 percent.[34] But the United States continues to record the highest rate of teen pregnancy in the industrialized world. The birthrate for teens in the U.S. is nearly double that of Canada, four times that of France and Germany, and more than eight times that of Japan.[35]

When asked why they get pregnant or get someone pregnant, most teens blame lack of motivation to use birth control, alcohol and drugs,

REASONS TEENS GIVE FOR GETTING PREGNANT OR GETTING SOMEONE PREGNANT	
Lack of sufficient motivation to avoid pregnancy	23.2%
Parents not paying attention	22.4%
Influence of alcohol and drugs	22.3%
Poor morals and values	14.8%
Birth control or protection too hard to get	7.9%
The media	7.9%

Adapted from The National Campaign to Prevent Teen Pregnancy, "With One Voice: America's Adults and Teens Sound Off About Teen Pregnancy: A National Survey," April 2001. Chart 6, p. 10.

or permissive parents. Teens sometimes blame their sexual partner for an unwanted pregnancy, but the truth is that intercourse requires two.

What Kinds of Contraceptives Do Young Adults Use, and How Much Can We Trust Them?

Among teens ages 15 to 19 who use contraception, the most popular form is the female birth control pill. In second place is the male condom. Injectable or implant forms of hormonal contraception are used by a smaller number, as are spermicidal foams, jellies, suppositories, and film.[36] Growing in popularity are the contraceptive ring and patch. They release hormones into the blood that mimic the preventive action of birth control pills, but daily pill-taking is not necessary. The ring is inserted in the vagina monthly. The patch is placed on the skin weekly.

"Withdrawal" and periodic abstinence ("the rhythm method") are used rarely, and for good reason. Neither method is reliable.

Withdrawal means removing the penis from the vagina before ejaculation. It is difficult for the male to achieve, and the secretions that exit the penis before orgasm contain sperm that can cause pregnancy. Couples who rely on periodic abstinence, or timing intercourse to avoid predicted fertile periods in the woman's cycle, are eventually called parents—for two reasons. First, sperm can survive in female reproductive organs for as long as seven days. Second, female cycles vary, and an egg can be released from an ovary at virtually any time during the cycle.

As for trusting your chosen method, the success mostly depends on you. Condoms themselves fail in less than 2 percent of cases, but the failure rate for condom *users* is 12 percent.[37] The most common error? Neglecting or forgetting or "not bothering" to use a condom every time, for every act of sexual intercourse. Other common contraceptive failures include taking birth control pills at the wrong time, forgetting to take them, or missing a doctor's appointment for a shot or implant.

Are Injections and Implants Better Than Birth Control Pills?

Ask your doctor. Young adults can safely use injected contraceptives, which are given at two- or three-month intervals. The most commonly used implant consists of 6 time-release hormone capsules. Inserted under the skin, the implant can prevent pregnancy for as long as five years. Both injections and implants approach 100 percent effectiveness in preventing pregnancy. They cannot, however, prevent disease transmission. (Only male and female condoms can do that.) Users of implants and injections needn't remember to take a pill every day, but appointments with a health care provider must be kept regularly. The initial cost is greater than pills, but it averages about the same over time.

What Should We Do if the Condom Breaks or if a Pill Is Forgotten, Lost, or Delayed?

If a birth control accident happens, don't despair. Emergency contraceptive pills are available and effective if taken within three days of unprotected vaginal intercourse. They prevent fertilization of an egg cell by a sperm cell, or block a fertilized egg from implanting in the uterus. They will not abort an established pregnancy. Emergency contraception is available from doctors, family planning clinics, and other health care providers. In California, emergency pills are available from pharmacists without a prescription. For a source in your area, call 1-800-230-PLAN or 1-888-NOT-2-LATE.

If you are having sex, it's a good idea to get emergency contraceptive pills before an accident happens. That way you'll be ready for the unexpected. You'll be able to prevent pregnancy within the 72-hour period the treatment requires—even on weekends, holidays, and vacations, when seeing a doctor might be difficult.

With Contraceptives So Easy to Get, Why Doesn't Everybody Use Them?

One of the best sources of contraception in many communities is the local Planned Parenthood clinic. "Planned Parenthood?" some young people ask. "Why should I go there? I'm not planning a family. That's something old people do, after they get married." But, whether they realize it or not, teens who are having sex are planning a family. They are planning for a family to start before they want it to.

Planned Parenthood doctors and nurses hear many reasons why teens don't use contraception . . . and later wish they had:

- "I wasn't thinking ahead. Having a baby was something I was going to do someday, but I just didn't think it could happen now."
- "Pregnancy was something that happened to bad girls, girls who sleep around and don't go to church. I think of myself as good, and I was only having sex with my boyfriend, not a lot of guys."
- "I felt so dumb and awkward trying to put on a condom. I thought my girlfriend would laugh at me."
- "I didn't think I needed to worry about wearing a condom. Isn't it the girl's job to think about stuff like that?"

Some young people say they feel too embarrassed to buy condoms or ask a doctor for contraceptive pills. Girls sometime say they didn't want to anger their boyfriends by insisting on contraception. Some teens say planning for sex would be a sin, but just letting it happen . . . somehow . . . isn't.

Teens who become fathers and mothers before their time often realize too late that their reasons didn't make sense. Admitting an unwanted pregnancy scores a lot higher on the embarrassment scale than requesting or buying contraceptives, and surely a boyfriend who won't use contraception to protect himself and his partner isn't worth having. Sexual intercourse is sexual intercourse, whether it's planned or not. For those who feel guilty, failing to plan for their own protection can't and won't diminish the guilt.

While more teens are now using contraception the first time they have sex, too many are failing to stay alert over the long haul. For the most recent intercourse, 31 percent of girls report that they were unprotected, and one third of sexually active teens do not use contraception consistently (every day for the pill; every intercourse for the condom).[38] The result? Parenthood—planned by not planning.

Can We Get Birth Control Pills Without Our Parents Knowing?

In April 2001, the Center for Reproductive Law and Policy issued a state-by-state report. At that time, no law in any state required notification of parents or parental permission for contraception.[39] The center noted, however, that proposals for such laws occasionally arise, and some laws or policies may have changed since that time. Also, some doctors may not be willing to prescribe contraception without parental permission for those under 16 or 18. Physicians with that policy should, however, refer teens to other physicians who will comply. To get up-to-date information about your community, call your local health department or the Planned Parenthood national hot line at 1-800-230-PLAN.

Do Gay or Lesbian Couples Need to Use Condoms?

Yes. The AIDS virus and many other disease-causing organisms pass from one person to another in body fluids, which may include semen, vaginal secretions, or menstrual blood. Contact with sores or lesions on the skin of the mouth, anus, or genitals may also transmit some diseases. Men who have anal or oral sex with men should always wear condoms. Women who have oral, anal, or vaginal contact with women should use a dental dam, as should heterosexual men performing oral sex on women. A dental dam is a piece of latex about five inches (12.5 centimeters) square that is worn by patients when dentists work on their teeth. Dental dams are available in medical supply stores, or they can be ordered online. For both gays and lesbians, latex gloves can prevent transmission of many (but not all) diseases when hands come in contact with mouth, anus, or genitals.

Coalition for Positive Sexuality

What Is a Hookup? Is It a Good Idea?

Researcher Elizabeth Paul defines a hookup as "a sexual encounter, usually lasting only one night, between two people who are strangers or brief acquaintances."[40] The partners are essentially anonymous and rarely if ever see each other again. Older terms for hookups are "casual sex" and "one-night stand." Alcohol or drugs usually play a part. The more intoxicated the partners are, the greater their sexual involvement.

Hookups attract people who fear attachment and seek short-term thrills. Such persons are impulsive, rebellious, and have little concern for personal safety. In her study of college students, Paul found that those who avoid hookups are honest in their dealings with others, comfortable with intimacy, and self-confident, even if they aren't the center of attention. Hookup seekers, on the other hand, have low self-esteem that dips even lower after hookups that they regret.

What Can We Do to Have a Good Sex Life?

The answer may surprise you. Stay in school. Researchers find that people who get an education through the college level have fewer sexual problems than those who stop their education earlier. The differences were especially great for women who don't earn their high school diplomas. They were almost twice as likely as university graduates to experience low levels of sexual desire.

Researchers in Illinois and New Jersey studied survey results from more than 3,000 people ages 18 to 59. They found that those who experienced poor physical or emotional health or had bad experiences in past sexual relationships were prone to problems such as lack of desire, difficulty getting aroused, inability to achieve orgasm, anxiety about sexual performance, or lack of pleasure in sex.[41]

As with any study of this kind, there's the problem of which came first. Do people who get an education achieve sexual health, or do sexually healthy people stay in school? Or does some third factor favor both school attendance and sexual performance? The experts can't say what causes what, only that the two go together.

Why Sex? Why Now?

· · · · ·

So many people are seeking long, romantic walks on the beach,
it's a wonder they haven't worn away our Continental Shelf.
COLIN MCENROE

· · · · ·

Though not everyone finds the perfect partner for romantic walks on the beach, nearly everyone has sex at some time in life. So the big question is not "if" but "when, where, and with whom?" Many factors influence the decision to have sex. It's an individual choice, of course, and people make it for many different reasons.

Young men often say they want sex to see what it is like or to experience the physical sensations that it provides. Young women usually say that they are "in love" or want to please a partner. Peers influence both females and males, but often indirectly. "Friends may not twist your arm or nag you to have sex," one male high school student revealed, "but you know it's expected if you want to be popular."

Sometimes the pressure is to "fit in" or be "one of the crowd." In other cases, the pressure is just the opposite: to stand out from the crowd and be special for doing something others haven't. Either way, the pressure can rob young adults of their right to choose for themselves. Fortunately, the years of severe peer pressure usually end around age 18. When people enter adulthood, they become more comfortable "inside their own skins." They worry less about what others think and begin to understand and value their personal uniqueness more.

For that reason, many people in their teens decide to save sex for adult life. They know that sexual activities can carry a heavy price— such as emotional hurt, unwanted pregnancy, or sexually transmitted diseases.

The risks of sex seem to go along with other kinds of risks that tempt young people. Studies show that those who choose sex early in the teen years are also more likely to:

- hang out with friends who are also having sex.
- use drugs, alcohol, or both.
- stay away from church.
- drop out, skip school, or get poor grades in school.
- fight with their parents.[42]

In a 1999 study, 19 percent of girls and 31 percent of boys reported using alcohol or drugs during their last intercourse.[43] In one study, 78 percent of teen girls said that it was "easier to have sex" when using alcohol or other drugs.[44] In a 1995 report, young adults who drank frequently, smoked cigarettes, or used marijuana were two to three times more likely to be sexually active than those who didn't.[45]

Communication with parents is a big factor. One study found that when teens thought their mothers expected them to stay virgins they did.[46] A national study discovered that students who discussed AIDS and other sexually transmitted diseases with their parents used protection (for example, a condom) more often than did those who didn't have such conversations with their families.[47]

One high school sophomore (we'll call him Ethan) compiled the following list after taking an informal survey at his school. Ethan calls it the "Top Twenty (DUMB!) Reasons to Have Sex."

20. If I let myself get "carried away," it will "just happen."
19. I can get even with person A (who dumped me) by having sex with person B.
18. If I have sex with person A, I can make person B jealous.
17. I'm the only one who hasn't tried it.
16. It will make me feel important or grown-up.
15. It's cool.
14. If I have sex with him (or her), he (or she) will love me.
13. I want to fit in with the popular crowd.
12. My body is screaming for release!
11. Everyone else is doing it.

10. I want to know what it's like.

9. If I don't do it now, I may never get another chance.

8. If I don't, I'll lose him or her.

7. I'm too old to still be a virgin.

6. My friend said it's great. I should try it.

5. You can't get pregnant the first time (during your period . . . between periods . . . when you do it standing up . . . etc.).

4. I'm lonely (tired, bored, depressed).

3. I'm drunk, high, stoned—so what the heck!

2. It looks so great in the movies and on TV.

1. We're in love.

If these reasons strike you as missing the mark, you've got the idea. While sexual sharing between committed partners is fundamental, casual, unplanned, and frivolous sex can hurt, even kill.

Although Ethan's list captures the chaos of muddled thinking about sex, he missed a destructive situation that injures more young adults than most people realize. Some teens are forced, threatened, or cajoled into having sex against their will. Intercourse occurs "under pres-

sure"—either physically forced or compelled by arguments, nagging, intimidation, or repeated insistence.

More than one third of all teens say they have done something sexual—or felt pressure to do something sexual—that they did not feel ready to do.[48] In one study, one fifth of 14-year-old girls who had had sex reported that they had been pressured the first time they had intercourse and during their most recent intercourse.[49] One in four teen girls says her first intercourse was voluntary, but unwanted.[50] (If it was unwanted, was it truly voluntary?)

Physically forced sex is rape. Mentally and emotionally pressured sex goes by different names, but it's just as dangerous. If you think there's a chance that someone will make you have sex—or if it has already happened—see a counselor or doctor immediately! You may want to share your secret with a friend your own age, but realize that he or she is not in a position to help you. Only a responsible adult can, but sometimes even parents or teachers don't listen or understand. If your first cry for help fails, try again. Sex that you don't want and feel you can't escape can do serious harm.

CHAPTER FIVE

ABOUT WRONGS
AND RISKS

Sex can be the highest and smoothest place of going,
the utmost of being together, the least of loneliness any human
being can find. But sex can also be an agony and wanting. Hurting
and being hurt. And the endless waiting for what never is reached.

• DOROTHY WALTER BARUCH •

Are There Any Rights and Wrongs When It Comes to Sex?

Says Deborah M. Roffman, author of *Sex and Sensibility*:

I hear young people say that there are no objective or absolute standards and that people must decide for themselves what is right and wrong. Nonsense!!! Core human values—honesty, integrity, responsibility, mutuality, caring, respect for life and liberty—are absolute. Certain acts, such as rape, sexual harassment, and child molestation, are *always* wrong because they violate these values. Other sexual acts, when they violate these core values, can also be considered immoral. For example, if someone lies to another person to manipulate them into engaging in a sexual act, or if a couple has sexual intercourse with no thought or care about pregnancy or sexually transmitted infections, they are also ignoring or violating moral values. . . .

In our society, we have strong social taboos and laws prohibiting incest, rape, abuse of children, sexual intercourse with a minor (usually defined as under age 16), and producing or distributing certain kinds of pornography. These behaviors are wrong because they misuse or demean sex and are harmful to the individuals involved.[1]

I Have Some Pretty Weird Sexual Thoughts Sometimes. Am I Normal?

Fantasies involving several partners or exotic situations are common and perfectly normal. Other fantasies may signal a problem. Says David Osborne, a psychologist at the Mayo Clinic in Scottsdale, Arizona:

Unhealthy sexual behaviors generally involve recurrent intense fantasies, urges, or behaviors involving non-human objects, suffering or humiliation, children, or non-consenting partners. Some people cannot become aroused unless they imagine or act out such fantasies. In these situations, consulting a health care professional is strongly advised.[2]

Some of the thoughts or urges that might send you to a counselor include exhibitionism (a desire to expose your genitals in public), pedophilia (a sexual interest in children), and sadomasochism (a desire to inflict pain on others or on oneself). If you are using other people for your own sexual pleasure with no regard for their health or well-being, then you should seek help. Sexual thoughts that dominate one's life or feature controlling others are indications of trouble. If you feel conflict between your moral and religious beliefs and your sexual behavior, see a physician or counselor.

What Is Sexual Abuse? What Should I Do if It Happens to Me?

The American Medical Association defines sexual abuse as "the engagement of a child in sexual activities for which the child is developmentally unprepared and cannot give informed consent. Child sexual abuse is characterized by deception, force, or coercion."[3] Specific abusive acts may include intimate touching or oral contact, showing the genitals, forced masturbation, or penetration of the mouth, anus, or vagina by mouth, penis, or fingers. Involving a young person in prostitution, pornography, or sex "rituals" is also abuse. Abuse by a family member, including a stepparent, is incest.

An adult has power over a young person. That power can be misused to trick, coax, or threaten a child into performing sexual acts and keeping them secret. The child feels manipulated, confused, and ashamed. Abuse survivors come to believe that others control their lives. Abuse robs them of their freedom to act independently and to make their own choices. Feelings of helplessness and hopelessness erode coping skills and lessen their ability to protect themselves from further abuse.

Sexual abuse in childhood often leads to sexual risk taking in the teen years. Anita Raj at Boston University's School of Public Health

This billboard is a public service reminder—and warning.

studied over 1,600 high school students from Massachusetts ages 15 to 17. She found that 30 percent of young women and 9 percent of young men had experienced sexual contact against their will. Abused females were more likely to have been younger at their first intercourse, had three or more sexual partners in their lifetimes, and were twice as likely to have become pregnant. Young men who had been abused had more sex partners, used alcohol during intercourse, and were more likely to report having made someone pregnant. Raj concluded that "both males and females with a history of sexual abuse report higher sexual risk taking than those without a history of sexual abuse."[4]

Abuse in childhood leads to continued abuse in adulthood if it is not stopped. Jeremy Coid of St. Bartholomew's Hospital studied the medical records of more than 1,200 women. Those who had unwanted sexual intercourse before age 16 faced a triple risk of domestic violence as adults, including severe beatings. Odds of rape as adults tripled, too.[5]

Breaking the cycle of repeated sexual violence and repeated victimization requires courage. The first step toward recovery is to tell the truth. The secrecy that shields the criminal abuser must be broken. Raj advises, "To both adults and children we say that abuse is *never* the fault of victims. It is not their behavior and they cannot be held accountable for the behavior. It is *always* the perpetrator's fault."[6]

If sexual abuse has happened—or is happening—to you, seek help from legal, social, and counseling services. The national toll-free hot line number for rape, incest, and abuse is 1-800-656-HOPE.

Is It OK for My Boyfriend or Girlfriend to Hit Me?

No. Physical violence is never acceptable in any relationship. It must not be tolerated between parents and children, husbands and wives, or with dates, friends, acquaintances, or strangers. Yet it occurs all too often. A 2001 survey of more than 80,000 high school students in Minnesota in grades 9 to 12 found that 9 percent of the girls and 6 percent of the boys had experienced violence or rape from a date.[7] In the United States each year, approximately 1.3 million women and 835,000 men are physically assaulted by their sexual partners.[8]

The victims of such violence seldom tell anyone about the attack, however, because they:

- blame themselves;
- accept violence as a normal part in a relationship;

- fear parental disapproval; or
- believe it won't happen again. (It will!)

If someone strikes or harms you or forces you to have sex, end the relationship, stay away from that person, and ask for help from a parent, teacher, counselor, minister, or other adult that you trust. The national toll-free hotline number for rape, incest, and abuse is 1-800-656-HOPE.

What's the Difference Between Sexual Assault and Rape?

Under the law, indecent assault is any unwanted touching, forcing someone to watch pornography, or forcing masturbation. Rape means the penetration of mouth, anus, or vagina with a penis or other object without consent. Consent means agreement freely given. A person cannot agree freely if threatened with force or fear of harm—either to self or to someone else. Legal consent is also impossible for someone who is drugged, unconscious, drunk, or mentally incompetent. Consent cannot be given if the person is deceived about the nature or purpose of the act—for example, when an unethical therapist claims sexual intercourse is part of the treatment. Statutory rape is having sexual intercourse with someone under a certain age (usually 16). Such a minor is considered too young to consent freely.

In 2000, 261,000 persons in the United States were victims of rape, attempted rape, or sexual assault.[9] Every two minutes, somewhere in America, someone is sexually assaulted.[10] One out of every 6 American women have been the victims of an attempted or completed rape in their lifetime. A total of 17.7 million women have been rape victims.[11]

While there are no reliable annual surveys of sexual assaults on children, the Justice Department has estimated that one sixth of rape victims are younger than 12.[12] The younger you are, the more likely an attacker is to be a family member or someone you know. Between ages 12 and 17, one in five attackers is a family member and nearly two thirds are acquaintances or friends.[13] The risk of rape is highest between ages 16 and 19.[14] Girls in this age group are four times more likely to be sexually attacked than other women. Two thirds of rape victims know their attacker.[15] Fewer than one in three rapes and sexual assaults are reported to law enforcement officials.

Can a Male Be Raped? One in every six males is sexually abused in childhood.[16] In 1999, one out of every ten rape victims were male.[17] Nearly three million American men have experienced rape or sexual assault in their lifetime.[18]

Rape of men by men is more common than female-male rape, but the difference isn't as large as you might expect. Acquaintances or friends inflicted the most abuse (73 percent), but 16 percent involved strangers and 11 percent involved family members.[19] It's a myth that homosexual men rape or abuse younger males. The American Medical Association reports that 98 percent of men who rape boys say they are heterosexual.[20] Rapists tend to be known to their victims, but are not usually family members. Male rapes typically occur outside the home and happen more than once.

Men who are sexually abused as children often suffer from negative thoughts about themselves and low self-esteem. They may have trouble developing and keeping satisfying adult relationships. Victims of male-on-male abuse show higher levels of violence in their adult relationships than males who are not abused. Victims of female-male abuse are in danger of becoming sex offenders.

If you are a victim of rape or sexual abuse, report the crime and seek help. Your future depends on it.

 **What Is Date Rape?** Date rape is sex forced upon you by someone you have gone out with voluntarily. It may happen on a first date or in a long-term relationship. It's the most common kind of rape, accounting for 70 to 80 percent of calls to rape crisis centers. Among college women, 14 percent say they have experienced date rape. For more than half of them, drugs or alcohol were involved.[21]

Certain drugs have a reputation as date rape drugs. One is GHB (for gamma hydroxybutyrate), known by the street names Liquid Ecstasy, Liquid X, Grievous Bodily Harm, and Georgia Home Boy. It is an odorless, colorless liquid that can be mixed into a drink. Many boys believe that GHB will make a girl want to have sexual intercourse and that she will not remember what she did later. In truth, the drug can cause a temporary "high," hallucinations, and memory loss. It can also halt breathing, cause a loss of consciousness, and kill within minutes—especially if combined with alcohol.

Another so-called date rape drug is rohypnol, also known by the street names Roofies, Roach, R-Z, Rope, Stupifi, and Shays. The small white tablets can be given by mouth or ground up and added to a drink. Rohypnol brings on drunkenness, deep sleep, breathing difficulties, and blackouts that can last for a day. If overdosed or mixed with alcohol, the drug can kill.

A poster from the "My Strength Is Not for Hurting" series from the Men Can Stop Rape organization.

A third so-called date rape drug is ketamine, or "Special K." It comes as a liquid, powder, or tablet. It disturbs balance, distorts time sense, and interferes with the ability to communicate. It brings on blurred vision, disorientation, trembling, hallucinations, and loss of consciousness.

It's important for victims of date rape and violence to seek immediate help. Calling 911 and going to a hospital can save a life, and seeing a doctor can prevent pregnancy. Long-term counseling may also help avert the increased risk of eating disorders, thoughts of suicide, and other psychological outcomes of date violence.[22]

Legal action is important to stop rapists from raping again. Young men who force sex or give date rape drugs to young women face criminal charges, trial, and imprisonment.

What Can I Do to Avoid Date Rape?

- Choose your friends and your dates carefully. Pick the parties you attend with equal care.
- Make sure someone you trust knows where you are going and when you will return. Phone home if your plans change.
- Go to a party with a friend, and agree to look out for each other.
- Have a plan for getting home if your date lets you down. Have a "Come pick me up, no questions asked" agreement in place with a parent or friend. Carry money and the telephone number of a taxi company with you at all times.
- Don't leave open drinks on tables or counters, and don't drink from communal punch bowls. Ask for a drink in a sealed bottle or can and open it yourself.

STRAIGHT TALK ABOUT RAPE

For MALES:

The Myth	The Truth
"No" means "maybe." She'll want to have sex if I get her drunk or "in the mood."	"No" means "no," and you can be prosecuted for rape if you ignore it.
"She must want it because she is wearing sexy clothes."	Sexy clothes to you are just fashion to her. Draw no conclusions from style of dress.
"She's had sex with me before. Why should now be any different?"	If she says no this time, she means no. Her agreement in the past does not necessarily mean she is ready to agree now.
"I know she wants it. She's just leading me on."	If she says she does not want sex, believe her. She knows her own mind. You do not.

For FEMALES:

The Myth	The Truth
"I must have led him on." "It's my fault." "I must have asked for it."	If you said no, you didn't lead him on. It is not your fault. No woman deserves forced sex against her will. He committed a crime, and nothing you did can absolve him of guilt for that crime.
"It's to be expected. Men are just like that."	Men are not animals. Society expects them to control their desires, and forced sex is not expected, normal, or in any way justified.
"If I tell about the forced sex or make a fuss over it, I'll lose him as a boyfriend."	Any man who rapes a woman is not worth keeping. Get out of the relationship immediately.
"Unwanted sex happens in all relationships. It's just something I'll have to learn to like."	Good relationships are based on mutual respect. No truly loving relationship involves force, violence, or coercion. Sex should be shared, never compelled.
"It's my fault because I was drunk or high."	Your state of intoxication is irrelevant. Your refusal is to be accepted and respected no matter what your physical or mental impairment.

- Don't take drugs or drink alcohol. These substances impair your judgment and make you vulnerable.
- Don't go places where sexual activity is expected.
- Have a handy "turn-off" line in mind. Something like, "Be careful. I'm a mud wrestler and I wouldn't want to hurt you," or "My brother is a hit man for the Mafia," can sometimes defuse a difficult situation.
- Wear several layers of clothes that are hard to get off. That may slow things down enough for you to regain control.
- Say "No" and mean it. Use an assertive tone of voice. Leave no room for doubt about your intentions.
- If you have had sex with your date in the past, discuss your feelings with your date. Point out that saying "Yes" once does not mean that you intend to say "Yes" again, on every occasion, or in the future.

If you think you've been drugged, ask someone to call 911 to request an ambulance. You may need immediate medical attention.

Why Do Young People Take Risks?

No one can answer that question fully, but it's important to remember that risk taking can be a positive force in life. Exploration is a normal part of growing up. Experimentation is a way of testing oneself and the world. Pushing the boundaries helps young people determine who they are, what strengths they possess, and where they can contribute to their culture. Risk taking is essential to gaining independence from parents and assuming adult levels of freedom and responsibility.

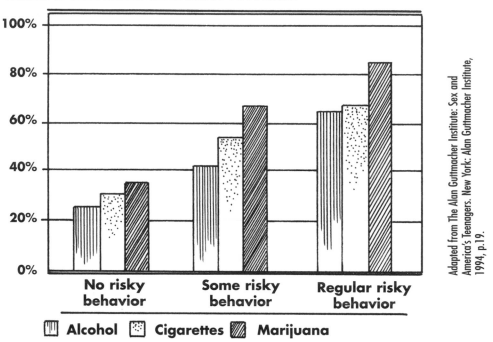

Adapted from The Alan Guttmacher Institute: Sex and America's Teenagers. New York: Alan Guttmacher Institute, 1994, p.19.

▥ Alcohol ▨ Cigarettes ▧ Marijuana

Early sex goes along with other dangerous behaviors such as using alcohol, cigarettes, and marijuana.

Risk taking has its dark side, however, when young people take chances that can permanently and seriously impair their health and well-being. Two reasons frequently given for high-level risk taking are underestimating the risk and failing to fear its outcomes. For example, a young driver who speeds on an icy road may not realize how likely an accident is under such conditions. Or, the driver may unconsciously believe that no harm can come from the action. In sexual risk-taking situations, young people who know about diseases, unwanted pregnancy, and emotional hurt act as if they didn't know. They convince themselves that the risks are not for them, or that they are lucky enough or special enough to escape the consequences that others suffer.

Risky behaviors tend to go together, perhaps because young people experiment in several different arenas at the same time. In a 1995 study, for example, students who drank frequently, smoked cigarettes, or used marijuana were two to three times more likely to be sexually active. Alcohol users more frequently reported multiple sex partners.[23]

One factor stands out among others as a possible explanation: overconfidence. Adam Goodie at the University of Georgia asked people to make bets based on how sure they felt of their answers to trivia questions. People risked large amounts when they felt certain they "knew it all," and continued to do so, even when their confidence proved ill founded. The teen years are a time of high expectations for the future. Teens may believe they are in control when, in fact, they are not. "People are really willing to take risks when they're highly confident in their own knowledge, even when it's a bad idea," says Goodie.[24]

Maybe a healthy measure of self-doubt is a good thing.

What Are My Chances of Getting a Sexually Transmitted Disease?

Four million American teens—about one in every four of those who have sex—get a sexually transmitted disease (STD) every year. By the age of 24, one in every three people contract an STD.[25] The World Health Organization estimates annual infection rates worldwide at 12 million for syphilis, over 60 million for gonorrhea, and more than 80 million for chlamydia.

Worldwide, half of HIV infections (the virus that causes AIDS) occur among people younger than 25.[26] At the end of 2000, nearly half a million Americans were living with HIV/AIDS. A similar number had died from it.[27] The number of AIDS cases diagnosed that year in the United States was nearly 25,000.[28]

Females are more susceptible to STDs than males. Adolescent girls and young adult women (compared with older women) have a characteristic called cervical ecotopy. Cells that line the inside of the cervix extend onto its outer surface. These cells are highly vulnerable to infections. Some researchers think that the thinner cervical mucus produced by young women makes them more vulnerable, too.

What STDs Are Most Common?

Probably some you've never heard of. First, at more than five million new cases annually in the United States, is infection by the human papillomavirus (HPV)—not to be confused with HIV, the virus that causes AIDS. HPV causes genital warts and cervical cancer. In second place is trichomoniasis (see pages 79–81) at five million, with the bacterial infection chlamydia coming in third.

What is The Human Papillomavirus, and How Is It Treated?

The human papillomavirus (HPV) is the most common sexually transmitted virus in America.[29] About one in every hundred adults has visible genital warts from the virus, but 15 percent or more carry the infection without symptoms.[30] Somewhere between 10 and 46 percent of sexually active women are infected at some point in time, and the lifetime risk may run as high as 70 percent. Infection rates are particularly high among people in their 20s.[31]

More than 100 different types of HPV are known.[32] About 20 to 30 of them can infect the genitals.[33] Individuals may be infected with more than one HPV type. Two types identified as HPV-16 and HPV-18 are found in nearly all women who get cancer of the cervix.[34] HPV is also the most common cause of penile and anal cancers.

Treatments can remove external warts, which may be painful or itchy. Skin creams and gels are sometimes used, as are drugs that bolster the immune system's attack on the virus. Warts may be removed surgically, with an electric current, or by freezing with liquid nitrogen. Doctors may apply certain acids and chemicals that destroy the warts. Although many people can expect a full recovery in six months or less, some 25 to 50 percent of patients have recurring episodes.[35] Most HPV infections clear within a year, and 92 percent within two years.[36] Treatment of visible warts does not reduce the risk of cervical cancer, but the disease can be diagnosed and treated early if women get regular Pap smears (see pages 81–83).

What Is Chlamydia, and How Is It Treated?

The bacterium *Chlamydia trachomatis* infects the genitals, anus, or eyes. It is the most frequently diagnosed bacterial STD in the developed world. In the United States, more than three million new cases occur annually.[37] Half the infected men and three quarters of women who have it show no symptoms.[38] That means millions of Americas carry chlamydia without knowing it.

Chlamydia causes pelvic inflammatory disease (PID) in women. PID is any type of inflammation of the upper female genital tract, including the uterus, Fallopian tubes, and ovaries. Chlamydia can also induce cervical cancer, ectopic pregnancy (pregnancy outside the uterus) and tubal infertility (a blockage of the Fallopian tubes that prevents the egg from traveling from the ovary to the uterus). A pregnant woman with chlamydia has a 50-50 risk of passing the infection on to her newborn child.[39] The infection can blind or kill an infant.

Chlamydia is treated with antibiotics. If you have chlamydia, your sexual partner(s) must be treated, to prevent reinfection or spreading the infection to other partners. Because chlamydia often shows no symptoms, it makes sense for anyone who is sexually active to be tested regularly. If your doctor doesn't give you a chlamydia test, ask for one.

What Is Syphilis, and How Is It Treated?

Syphilis is an infection by the bacterium *Treponema pallidum*. *Treponema* is a spirochete, or spiral-shaped microbe. It moves from one person to another during sexual contact. The first sign of an infection may be an ulcer or sore on the genitals, but the infection may take hold without causing any symptoms at all. The sore, if one appears, heals in a few weeks without treatment, but the infection is not gone. It spreads quickly through the bloodstream to all parts of the body. It then produces a rash on the palms of the hands and soles of the feet. Sometimes gray or white sores develop in the mouth or on the genitals. Other symptoms may include fever, headache, fatigue, loss of appetite, sore throat, muscle soreness, hair loss, and weight loss. A mini-epidemic of syphilis occurred in the late 1980s and early 1990s. The infection rate in the United States ran higher then than at any time since the antibiotic penicillin became available. In 2000 the syphilis infection rate dropped to an all-time low, but new cases continue to be reported in some areas, including certain counties in Illinois and North Carolina.[40]

Syphilis must be treated early. If left untreated, it attacks the nervous system and can cause heart failure, nerve deterioration, deafness, and blindness. The antibiotic penicillin is an effective treatment for syphilis. The sexual partners of syphilis patients need penicillin treatment, too.

What Is Gonorrhea and How Is It Treated?

In the United States, some 600,000 new infections with the bacterium *Neisseria gonorrhoeae* occur each year.[41] The disease is most often found in men ages 20 to 24 and women ages 15 to 19. The risk for African Americans in ten times greater than for whites.[42] Symptoms of ulcerations on the penis and painful urination are usually (but not always) obvious in men, prompting them to seek treatment. Women, however, often have the infection without knowing it. Untreated gonorrhea in women can cause pelvic inflammatory disease (PID), infertility, and ectopic pregnancy. People with gonorrhea are often infected with *Chlamydia* as well, so doctors recommend treatment for both simultaneously. Antibiotics can effectively treat gonorrhea. The sexual partners of gonorrhea patients need antibiotic treatment, too.

What Is Genital Herpes, and How Is It Treated?

There are a lot of herpes simplex viruses (HSV) around. Most people carry them. (The chicken pox virus is a herpes virus, for example.) However, only two types induce genital herpes. HSV-1 is the same virus that causes cold sores in the mouth. At one time, it was never associated with genital infections, but that has changed in recent years as the popularity of oral sex among teens has grown.

HSV-2 is transmitted only by genital contact. In up to 95 percent cases of recurrent herpes cases—in which ulcers erupt repeatedly over time—the cause is HSV-2.[43] Genital HSV-2 has been diagnosed in at least 45 million people in the United States.[44] In 1999 about half a million Americans saw their doctors for genital herpes.[45]

The most common symptom of HSV infection is painful ulcers on the mouth or genitals. The sores erupt because the virus invades the nerves that serve the skin. The virus remains there, even after drugs clear the outward signs of infection. Many infected people show no symptoms. Sores need not be visible for a person to be contagious. Viruses shed from healthy-looking skin can infect a partner.

Doctors prescribe antiviral drugs to clear symptoms and prevent ulcers from reappearing. They recommend condoms for both oral and genital sex to prevent infection, promote healing, and suppress outbreaks. People with HSV must avoid sexual contact entirely when symptoms are present. Their sexual partners need medical treatment, too.

Is Hepatitis Sexually Transmitted?

Several forms of hepatitis (inflammation of the liver) caused by viruses are spread through sexual activity. Hepatitis A is transmitted by contact of mouth with anus (or by fingers that touch the anus and the mouth). Hepatitis B is transmitted through the exchange of bodily fluids. A vaccine against this form is now required at public schools across the country. Hepatitis C is occa-

4. increasing use
5. withdrawal symptoms arising from attempts to quit

The sexual addict experiences all these symptoms. He or she wants to quit investing so much time, effort, and money in sex, but cannot. The consequences are dire—loss of friendships, work problems, sexual diseases, emotional turmoil, and more. The time spent seeking and indulging in sex makes other aspects of life unmanageable. In attempting to curb the addiction, the addict feels sick, lost, and empty. Impulsively, the addict seeks still more sex as an antidote to depression and hopelessness.

Experts argue about whether this condition is an addiction or a compulsion, but, as Kasl points out, to those who suffer from a misuse of sex, the label doesn't matter. She sees compulsion as an earlier stage of addiction, in which thoughts of "I can't survive without . . . ," I must have . . . ," and "I've got to . . . " dominate mind and behavior. When the behavior—initially undertaken to reduce tension—begins to control one's life, addiction has taken over. "Addiction is like having two sides—the addict side and the health side—engaging in a life-and-death struggle to control the inner world," Kasl writes.[50]

"Sexual behavior becomes compulsive when it begins to interfere with other aspects of a person's life," says Donald Williams, a psychologist at the Mayo Clinic in Rochester, Minnesota.[51] Compulsive sexual disorders can be treated with counseling and group therapy. Antidepressant medicines help some, while others find that learning positive nonsexual ways to cope with stress alleviates their symptoms. As a result, sexual addicts can begin to feel "normal" and develop the motivation needed to pursue life goals and dreams. Recovery from a sexual addiction requires time, patience, and effort, but it can save individuals and families from immeasurable pain.

Abstinence: The Debate That Isn't

· · · · ·

Science is our best hope of understanding the strange alchemy of lust that so disrupts our social lives.

CAMILLE PAGLIA
AUTHOR, *SEXUAL PERSONAE*

· · · · ·

If you've been living on Mars since infancy, you may not have heard that sexual activity carries with it the risk of pregnancy and sexually transmitted diseases. And, if you have been living in a cave on that planet with no access to books, magazines, TV, radio, or other human beings, you may have missed learning that abstinence (not having sex or "saving sex" for a later time) is the only surefire way to avoid both.

For everyone else, the debate is hardly a debate. If you want to prevent pregnancy and avoid some very nasty, potentially life-threatening bacteria and viruses, don't have sex. It's the simple "Just Say No" message, and some evidence suggests that

teens are acting on it. For many years, the number of U.S. high school students who had never had sexual intercourse fell just below half. In 1993 about 44 percent of boys and not quite 50 percent of girls remained virgins throughout high school. By 1997 the numbers had risen to more than half (52 percent of girls and 51 percent of boys). And, although the number declined for males in 1999, it still exceeded the numbers in 1993 and 1995.[52]

In one survey, nearly six in every ten teens said they thought sexual activity was not appropriate for people of middle school or high school age, even if protection against pregnancy and disease was used. In fact,

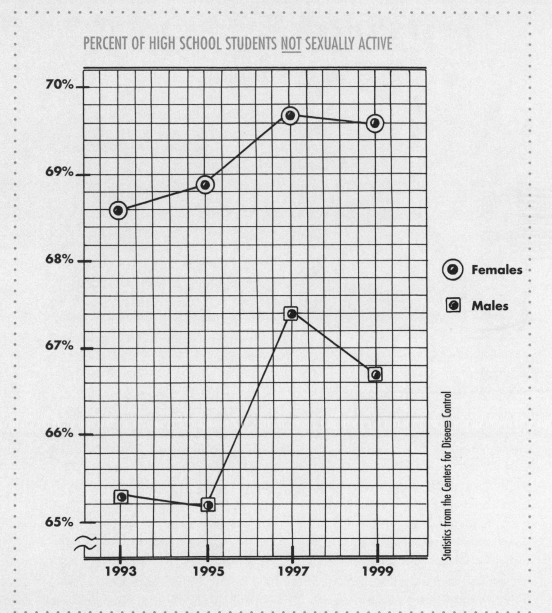

PERCENT OF HIGH SCHOOL STUDENTS <u>NOT</u> SEXUALLY ACTIVE

Statistics from the Centers for Disease Control

Females

Males

when you're a teenager,
life is full of positives...

don't let a
PREGNANCY TEST
be one of them.
The National Campaign to Prevent Teen Pregnancy
teenpregnancy.org

The National Campaign to Prevent Teen Pregnancy offers postcards teens can send to their friends. On the flip side this one says, "If you think birth control 'ruins the mood,' consider what a pregnancy will do to it."

87 percent of the respondents in that survey said they saw nothing embarrassing about admitting virginity.[53] In another survey, three out of every four teens said, "It's a good thing to make a conscious decision not to have sex until some later time," and nearly half said they had made that decision.[54]

The number of U.S. high school students who are *not* sexually active is growing. Today, two out of every three high school students are—now and within the last three months—abstinent, even if they have had sexual intercourse at some previous time in their lives. For some good reasons of their own, young adults are choosing to postpone sex. "I want to finish high school and go to college" says 15-year-old Amanda. "Getting pregnant or getting AIDS would mess up my life big time," she says. Jared, who's going with a girl he hopes to marry someday, says he's choosing abstinence, too. "We—Keisha and me—well, we just want to wait until we are married. We want sex to be something special, and we'd ruin it if we started messing around now." Caitlin, who's abstinent now but had intercourse with her boyfriend in the ninth grade and then broke up with him, says, "I just don't want to go through that hurt again. I cried for weeks after Chris and I split up, and I don't think I would have felt so lost and ashamed if we hadn't been having sex." John, who has had sex with both male and female partners, says he's avoiding sex for a while. "I feel confused about whether I'm gay or straight or bisexual," he admits. "I think I need to give myself some time to figure things out."

Between 1991 and 1997, the percentage of U.S. high school students who were virgins increased, as did the number of condom and birth control users among those who weren't. During that same period, the infection rate for gonorrhea dropped 35 percent among males and 11 percent among females ages 15 to 19. Teen pregnancy rates dropped, too.[55] Most young people understand that abstinence is a good idea for those who chose it. For those who don't, condoms are sold in supermarkets, drugstores, gas stations, public toilets, and online. More than half of young men are using condoms when they have intercourse, and nearly two thirds of women report condom use the last time they had intercourse. Protection against pregnancy and disease will improve as the numbers using condoms rise.

Of course, contraceptives are not 100 percent effective in preventing pregnancy, and none but the condom offers protection against disease. Still, contraceptives and condoms cut the physical risks of teen sex, if not the emotional ones. Psychologically, the hurt of a sexual relationship gone wrong hurts too many teens too deeply. Studies that link early intercourse with depression and suicidal thoughts give chill warning of the power that sex exerts in our lives.

When asked what advice they'd give a younger brother or sister or friend, 64 percent of teens answered, "Don't have sex until you're at least out of high school. But if you do, protect yourself against pregnancy and disease."[56] The wisdom of abstinence is not debatable. Neither is the wisdom of the condom.

IN CLOSING

If this book has a theme, it is this: Sex is about what's above the neck, not about what's below. The human brain is the most remarkable of all organs, capable of great love, caring, and commitment. It is also capable of turning the treasure of sexuality into ravage and ruin.

Scientist Victor S. Johnston is known for his research into the science of human emotions. He studies the brain's left hemisphere—the supposed rational and reasoning side—along with the silent and more mysterious right hemisphere, where our perceptions of the world as a unified whole are formed and processed. In simplest terms, we think with our left brain, but feel with our right.

Johnston's book *Why We Feel* offers a lot of information and ideas for the left brain, but for those who favor right hemisphere processing, Johnston wrote this poem in the style of a Shakespearean sonnet.[1] It ends this book as we began it—with an answer to the question, "**Sex? What's the big deal?**"

"Why We Feel" for the Right Hemisphere

What love is this that floods my conscious mind
and strips my senses of the waking day?
How can illusions such as this arise
in worthless mortals made from stars turned clay?

Ancestral struggles on an ancient earth
bequeathed emergent feelings to my brain.
Discordant voices from a distant past
now scream or whisper; anger, love, and pain.

Who planned this folly that we call a life?
Was it mere chance, or was it god divine?
Should we rejoice and taste each conscious hour,
or dull each senseless moment with red wine?

Such things men often ponder, but this I can decree.
When I had sex with Alice, it all made sense to me!

GLOSSARY

Abstinence. Not having intimate sexual contact, especially the complete avoidance of oral sex, anal, or vaginal intercourse.

Adolescence. The time period—typically between 11 and 19 years of age—of a person's mental and physical maturing toward adulthood.

AIDS (acquired immune deficiency syndrome). A sexually transmitted disease caused by a virus that attacks the body's immune system. AIDS is spread by contaminated body fluids and blood, usually through sexual contact or sharing unclean needles used to inject illegal drugs. AIDS is fatal.

Anal intercourse. The insertion of the penis into the anus.

Anus. The external opening of the large intestine.

Birth control. Avoiding pregnancy by using contraceptive protection during each act of intercourse. More at *Contraception.*

Bisexual. A person who engages in both heterosexual and homosexual relations or is sexually attracted to persons of both genders.

Breast. A mammary gland present in both sexes but milk-producing only in females after childbirth.

BV (bacterial vaginosis). An abnormal growth in the number of anaerobic bacteria in the vagina.

Cervix. Opening to the uterus located at the top of the vagina.

Chlamydia. A sexually transmitted disease caused by the bacterium *Chlamydia.*

Chromosome. Any one of the several structures in the nucleus of a cell that contains the genetic material DNA.

Circumcision. A surgical procedure to remove the loose flap, or foreskin, covering the end of the male penis. The word is also incorrectly applied to excision or mutilation of the female external genitalia.

Climax. See *Orgasm.*

Clitoris. A small sensitive bud of tissue located in the female labia just above the urinary and vaginal openings. It contains numerous nerve ends, and its stimulation produces sexual pleasure in females.

Conception. The union of the egg from the female and a sperm from the males. Also called fertilization.

Condom. A sheath of latex or similar material that fits over the penis and catches the semen released at ejaculation. Condoms are highly (but not totally) effective in preventing pregnancy and disease transmission.

Contraception. The prevention of pregnancy. Various methods include the condom, the contraceptive pill, diaphragm, implants, injections, intrauterine devices, and others.

Conversion therapy. See *Reorientation therapy.*

Date rape. Sexual penetration forced on the victim by a social companion.

Douche. A solution used to rinse the vagina; or the act of using such a solution.

Dyspareunia. Pain of the vulva, vagina, or lower abdomen experienced during sexual intercourse.

Ejaculation. When an erect penis releases semen during intercourse, masturbation, or sleep (see *Nocturnal emission*).

Embryo. The human organism from 48 hours after conception to the end of the eighth week of development.

Epididymis. A bundle of tubes atop the testicles, where sperm cells are stored as they mature.

Epididymitis. Inflammation of the epididymis.

Erectile dysfunction. Inability to achieve penile erection.

Erection. Temporary hardening, or stiffening, of the penis caused by increased blood flow into its spongy tissues.

Estrogen. A hormone produced by the female ovaries and by the adrenal glands in both males and females. Estrogen produces female sexual characteristics and helps regulate the menstrual cycle.

Fallopian tubes. Tubes that lie between the female ovaries and the uterus. The egg travels through these tubes and is usually fertilized there.

Female circumcision. Mutilation of the female genitals.

Fetus. Unborn human from eight weeks of development to birth.

Foreskin. The skin around the tip of the male penis.

Gay. A person whose sexual orientation is homosexual; specifically, a male who is homosexual. See *Lesbian.*

Gender dysphoria. Dissatisfaction with one's sex as defined by appearance or anatomy. See *Gender identity.*

Gender identity. A person's internal sense of being male or female.

Gene. A segment of the hereditary molecule DNA. The basic unit of inheritance.

Genetic. Inherited; passed from parents to their offspring.

Genitalia. (Also called genitals.) Human external sex organs.

Glans. Head, or end, of the penis.

Gonorrhea. A sexually transmitted disease caused by the bacterium *Neisseria gonorrhoeae.*

G-spot. An area of the vagina purported to be especially sensitive to sexual stimulation. Its existence is debated.

Gynecomastia. Enlargement of breasts in the male.

Hernia. A weakness of the muscular wall of the lower abdomen.

Herpes. A sexually transmitted disease that usually appears in the form of sores on the genitals.

Heterosexual. Sexual attraction to persons of the opposite gender, or a person who is thus attracted.

HIV (human immunodeficiency virus). The virus that causes the sexually transmitted disease AIDS.

Homosexual. Sexual attraction to persons of the same gender, or a person who is thus attracted.

Hormone. A substance produced in one part of the body that has an effect on another part of the body.

HPV (human papillomavirus). The virus that causes genital warts and most cervical cancers.

Hydrocele. Accumulation of fluid around a testicle.

Hymen. A thin piece of skin that may block or partially block the vaginal opening of some young females.

Hypogonadism. Small penis size in the male.

Impotence. See *Erectile dysfunction.*

Incest. Sexual activity between biological relatives or with a relative by marriage (such as a stepfather) who is not a spouse. Incest is illegal.

Intercourse. See *Sexual intercourse.*

Intersex. A person born with ambiguous genitalia, so that gender is not apparent from external anatomy.

Jock itch. A fungal infection of skin around the genitals.

Labia. The folds surrounding the vagina in the human female.

Lesbian. A female whose sexual orientation is homosexual.

Linkage. In genetics a pattern of inheritance in which characteristics appear to be inherited together because the genes that control them occur close together on the same chromosome.

Mastalgia. Breast pain.

Masturbation. Massaging the genitals to produce sexual stimulation in oneself or in a sexual partner (mutual masturbation).

Menarche. A girl's first menstrual period.

Menstruation. Shedding of the unfertilized egg and uterine lining of a nonpregnant female.

Mons (or mons pubis). In the human female, the mound where pubic hair grows.

Neurotransmitter. A chemical that carries an impulse from one nerve cell to another.

Nocturnal emission. Semen released from the penis of a sleeping male. Also called "wet dream."

Oral sex. Stimulating a partner's sexual organs with the mouth or tongue.

Orchitis. Inflammation of a testicle.

Orgasm. The moment of sexual stimulation when the nerve endings in the penis or clitoris produce a series of rapid impulses that the brain interprets as intense sexual pleasure.

Ovary. The internal reproductive organ of the female where egg cells mature. It is a hormone-producing organ.

Pap smear. The collection and microscopic examination of cells from the cervix to identify potentially cancerous changes.

Penis. The male organ that evacuates urine from the bladder and releases semen during sexual activity.

Pheromone. A chemical released by one individual that produces a behavioral response in another individual of the same species.

Pituitary. The gland at the base of the brain that makes and releases many hormones, including those that stimulate the production of sex hormones by the ovaries or testicles.

PMDD (premenstrual dysphoric disorder). PMS severe enough to interfere with school, work, or social activities.

PMS (premenstrual syndrome). A group of physical and emotional symptoms such as fluid retention, fatigue, irritability, depression, and headache that may occur in some women prior to the start of the menstrual flow.

Pornography. Sexually explicit written or visual material created for the purpose of sexual stimulation.

Pregnancy. In human females, the time (about 36 weeks) and processes that occur as a fertilized egg develops into an infant capable of independent life outside the uterus.

Premature ejaculation. Ejaculation that occurs before a male or his sex partner wants it to.

Prepuce. See *Foreskin.*

Priapism. A painful erection that lasts for hours or days.

Prostate gland. One of the semen-producing glands in the male.

Prostitute. A person who performs sex acts in exchange for food, money, drugs, protection, or some other gain.

Puberty. The stage and process of development (usually between ages 10 and 19) in which a child's body changes into an adult body and the reproductive system matures.

Pubic hair. Hair on the external genital area of both males and females.

Rape. Penetration of mouth, vagina, or anus with a penis or other object without consent.

Reorientation therapy. Counseling aimed at changing the sexual orientation of gay, lesbian, or bisexual people.

Reparative therapy. See *Reorientation therapy.*

Scrotum. Sac of skin that surrounds the male testicles.

Semen. The mixture of fluid and sperm cells that is propelled from a man's body during ejaculation.

Sex chromosome. A structure in the nucleus of cells that carries genes associated with sexual differentiation (typically, either a pair of X chromosomes in the female, or an X and a Y in the male.)

Sexual abuse. Engagement of a child in sexual activities.

Sexual assault. Any sexual activity forced on one person by another. See also *Rape* and *Date rape.*

Sexual intercourse. The insertion of the erect male penis into the vagina of a female partner or into the anus of either a male or female partner.

Sexuality. The sum of an individual's gender identity, sexual orientation, and sexual feelings, thoughts, attitudes, and behaviors.

Sexual orientation. A person's sexual preferences and partnerships with members of the same or opposite sex or both.

Smegma. A thick white curdy substance that collects under the foreskin in males and inside the labial folds of females.

Sperm. A male reproductive cell capable of uniting with a female egg at conception.

Spermicide. Any of several sperm-killing chemicals used in contraceptive foams, creams, jellies, and films.

STD (sexually transmitted disease). A disease that passes from one person to another by sexual contact (vaginal, oral, or anal).

Syphilis. The sexually transmitted disease caused by the spiral-shaped bacterium *Treponema pallidum.*

Testicles (or testis, plural *testes).* The male sexual organs contained within the scrotum that manufacture sperm and male sex hormones.

Testicular torsion. A painful twisting of the sperm cord that blocks blood flow to the testicles.

Testosterone. The hormone primarily responsible for sexual characteristics and development in the male (produced by the testicles) and for arousal and desire in both sexes (produced by the ovary and adrenal gland).

Transgender. A person who feels, looks, or behaves in ways typically associated with the opposite sex.

Transsexual. A person who has changed sexual characteristics and anatomy either surgically, through hormone treatments, or both.

Trichomoniasis. An infestation of the vagina by the one-celled organism *Trichomonas.*

Urethra. The internal tube that carries urine from the bladder to outside the body.

Urethral meatus. The opening at the tip of the penis through which urine and semen leave the male body.

Uterus. (Also called womb.) Muscular pear-shaped organ in the female that contains the developing embryo/fetus during pregnancy.

Vagina. Tube of muscular tissue in the female that lies between the outer vulva and the uterus.

Vaginismus. An involuntary tightening of the vaginal muscles that can make penetration difficult or impossible.

Vaginitis. Any itching or burning inflammation of the vagina and vulva.

Variocele. A knot of distended veins in the sperm cord above a testicle.

Virgin. A person who has never has sexual intercourse.

Vulva. External genital organs of the female.

Wet dream. See *Nocturnal emission.*

Withdrawal. The male attempting to pull his penis out of the female's vagina before he ejaculates. Not a form of birth control or disease prevention.

X-linked inheritance. Also called sex-linked inheritance. A characteristic or hereditary pattern associated with genes carried on the X chromosome.

Yeast infection. Abnormal growth of *Candida* or *Torulopsis* yeast species in the vagina.

FOR FURTHER INFORMATION

Books

American Medical Association. *Guide to Sexuality*. New York: Dell, 1996.

Bass, Ellen, and Kate Kaufman. *Free Your Mind: The Book for Gay, Lesbian, and Bisexual Youth*. New York: HarperPerennial Library, 1996.

Basso, Michael J. *The Underground Guide to Teenage Sexuality*. Minneapolis: Fairview Press, 1997.

Bell, Ruth, and others. *Changing Bodies, Changing Lives: A Book for Teens on Sex and Relationships*, 3rd ed. New York: Three Rivers Press, 1998.

Blum, Deborah. *Sex on the Brain: The Biological Differences between Men and Women*. New York: Penguin, 1997.

Bull, David. *Cool and Celibate? Sex and No Sex*. New York: HarperCollins, 1998.

Colapinto, John. *As Nature Made Him: The Boy Who Was Raised as a Girl*. New York: HarperCollins, 2000.

Crenshaw, Theresa L. *The Alchemy of Love and Lust: How Our Sex Hormones Influence Our Relationships*. New York: Pocket Books, 1997.

DiSpezio, Michael. *The Science of HIV*. Washington, D.C.: NSTA Press, 2000. (Comes with a 30-minute video.)

Drill, Esther, Heather McDonald, and Rebecca Odes. *DEAL WITH IT! A Whole New Approach to Your Body, Brain, and Life as a gURL*. New York: Pocket Books, 1999.

Endersbee, Julie K. *Healthy Sexuality: What Is It?* Mankato, MN: Lifematters Press, 2000.

Gordon, Sol. *How Can You Tell If You're Really in Love?* Avon, MA: Adams Media, 2001.

Johnson, Eric W. *Love and Sex in Plain Language*, 4th ed. New York: Bantam, 1988.

Kohl, James Vaughn. *The Scent of Eros: The Mysteries of Odor in Human Sexuality*. New York: Continuum Publishing, 1995.

Lieberman, E. James, and Karen Lieberman Troccoli. *Like It Is: A Teen Sex Guide*. Jefferson, NC: McFarland, 1998.

Palardy, Debra J. *Sweetie, Here's the Best Reason on the Planet to Say No to Your Boyfriend Even If You've Already Said Yes*. Pittsburgh: Dorrance, 2000.

Pogány, Susan Browning. *SexSmart: 501 Reasons to Hold Off on Sex*. Minneapolis: Fairview Press, 1998.

Vitkus, Jessica, and Marjorie Ingall. *Smart Sex*. New York: Pocket Books, 1998.

Walsh, Anthony. *The Science of Love: Understanding Love & Its Effects on Mind & Body*. Buffalo, NY: Prometheus Books, 1996.

Westheimer, Ruth. *Dr. Ruth's Encyclopedia of Sex*. News York: Continuum, 1994.

———. *Sex for Dummies*, 2nd ed. Foster City, CA: IDG, 2001.

White, Lee, Caesar Pacifici, and Mary Dilson. *The Teenage Human Body Operator's Manual*. Eugene, OR: Northwest Media, 1998.

Articles

Cowley, Geoffrey. "The Biology of Beauty." *Newsweek* (June 3, 1996), pp. 60–66.

Fischman, Josh, Jia-Rul Chong, and Roberta Hotinski. "Why We Fall in Love." *U.S. News & World Report* (February 7, 2000).

Horgan, John. "Sex, Flies, and Videotape." *Scientific American* (June 1997), pp. 26+.

Leland, John, Claudia Kalb, and Nadine Joseph. "The Science of Women and Sex," *Newsweek* (May 29, 2000), pp. 48+.

Lemley, Brad. "Isn't She Lovely?" *Discover* (February 2000), pp. 42–49.

Lemonick, Michael D. "Teens Before Their Time." *Time* (October 20, 2000), pp. 66–74.

Nash, Madeleine. "Science: The Personality Genes: Does DNA Shape Behavior?" *Time* (April 27, 1998), pp. 60+.

Peele, Stanton, and Richard DeGrandpre. "My Genes Made Me Do It." *Psychology Today* (July 17, 1995), pp. 50+.

Schnarch, David. "Joy with Your Underwear Down." *Psychology Today* (July 1994) 27: pp. 34+.

Yeoman, Barry. "Gay No More?" *Psychology Today* (April 1999), pp. 26–29+.

Web Sites

Scarleteen

www.scarleteen.com/sexuality/readiness.html

Are you ready for intercourse? Consult the Scarleteen checklist.

AVERT: Averting AIDS and HIV

www.avert.org

Good information on AIDS and links to many other AIDS information sites.

The National AIDS Hotline of the Centers for Disease Control and Prevention

www.ashastd.org/nah/

Information specialists are available 24 hours a day, 7 days a week, and can answer questions, provide referrals, and send free publications through e-mail and postal mail. Call 1-800-342-AIDS or (for Spanish) 1-800-344-7432.

The National STD Hotline

www.ashastd.org/NSTD/index.html

In addition to offering clinic referrals and written materials, health communication specialists answer questions about transmission, prevention, and treatment for diseases such as gonorrhea, chlamydia, HPV/genital warts, herpes, HIV, and others. Call 1-800-227-8922

Youth Shakers

www.youthshakers.org

An international youth Web site that includes information on youth programs and youth groups related to sexual health.

National Organization on Male Sexual Victimization

www.nomsv.org

The mission is to prevent abused boys from becoming abusive men.

Columbia University's Health Education Site

www.goaskalice.columbia.edu

This site will answer all those questions you're afraid to ask.

www.youth.org

YOUTH.ORG is a service run by volunteers, created to help gay, lesbian, bisexual, and questioning youth.

www.teenwire.com
The Planned Parenthood Federation of America teen site.

www.healthfinder.gov/justforyou/
The U.S. Department of Health and Human Services provides this site with links to information services specially designed for people of different ages and ethnic groups.

www.isna.org
The Intersex Society of North America promotes self-selection of gender for people born with ambiguous genitalia.

www.glnh.org
Call the Gay and Lesbian National Hotline 1-888-THE-GLNH evening and Saturday afternoon for peer counseling, information, and referrals.

www.notmenotnow.org
If you have questions about sex, or wonder if you are ready, this site presents the case for abstinence.

www.awarefoundation.org
The mission of the Adolescent Wellness and Reproductive Education Foundation (AWARE) is to educate and empower adolescents to make responsible decisions regarding their wellness, sexuality, and reproductive health.

http://ec.princeton.edu/
The Emergency Contraception Web site operated by the Office of Population Research at Princeton University and by the Association of Reproductive Health Professionals. Tells what to do if the condom broke or you forgot to take a pill.

Agencies and Organizations

Advocates for Youth
1025 Vermont Avenue, NW, Suite 200
Washington, D.C. 20005
www.youthresource.com/
Information on sexual health, sexual orientation, and links to helping organizations.

American Psychiatric Association
1400 K Street N.W., Washington, D.C. 20005
www.psych.org
Provides fact sheets on mental health, sexual development, and sexual orientation.

American Psychological Association
750 First Street, NE, Washington, D.C. 20002
www.apa.org
Provides fact sheets on mental health, sexual development, and sexual orientation.

Coalition for Positive Sexuality
PO Box 77212
Washington, D.C. 20013-7212
www.positive.org
Order the coalition's low-cost booklet, "Just Say Yes."

Colage
3543 18th St. #1
San Francisco, CA 94110
www.colage.org
An organization for the children of gay, lesbian, bisexual, and transgender parents.

Family Health International
P.O. Box 13950
Research Triangle Park, NC 27709
www.fhi.org
Family Health International works in 40 countries around the world and provides information to more than 200 countries. FHI provides more than 2,000 full text papers online, including information on family planning, sexually transmitted diseases, and women's health.

Harry Benjamin International Gender Dysphoria Association
1300 South Second Street, Suite 180
Minneapolis, MN 55454
www.hbigda.org
An association of professionals who understand and treat gender identity disorders.

International Planned Parenthood Federation
Regent's College
Inner Circle, Regent's Park
London NW1 4NS
United Kingdom
www.ippf.org
This is the world's largest voluntary organization in the field of sexual health and reproduction. At work in 180 countries.

Kaiser Family Foundation
2400 Sand Hill Road
Menlo Park, CA 94015
www.kff.org
Check out the Foundation's SexSmarts Web site, a public information partnership with *Seventeen* magazine.

Men Can Stop Rape
P.O. Box 57144
Washington, D.C. 20037
www.mencanstoprape.org
Offers a newsletter by e-mail and a magazine. Trains speakers for the prevention of sexism and sexual violence.

National Association for Research and Therapy of Homosexuality
16633 Ventura Boulevard, Suite 1340
Encino, CA 91436
www.narth.com
Promotes conversion therapy for homosexuals who wish to change orientation.

National Campaign to Prevent Teen Pregnancy
1776 Massachusetts Avenue NW, Suite 200
Washington, D.C. 20037
www.teenpregnancy.org
Take the weekly teen survey on their Web site and learn how to avoid pregnancy.

North American Society for Pediatric and Adolescent Gynecology
1015 Chestnut Street, Suite 1225
Philadelphia, PA 19107
www.naspag.org

Planned Parenthood Federation of America
810 Seventh Avenue
New York, NY 10019
www.plannedparenthood.org
Often the best source of information, contraception, and emergency services for teens and young adults. Call 1-800-230-PLAN.

Rape Abuse and Incest National Network (RAINN)
635-B Pennsylvania Ave., SE
Washington, D.C. 20003
www.rainn.org
RAINN offers free confidential counseling and support for victims or rape, incest, and abuse. Help is available 24 hours a day, from anywhere in the United States. Call toll-free 1-800-656-HOPE.

Search Institute
The Banks Building
615 First Avenue NE, Suite 125
Minneapolis, MN 55413
www.search-institute.org
Disseminates information that helps young people avoid risks and make healthy decisions.

Sexuality Information and Education Council of the United States (SIECUS)
130 West 42nd Street, Suite 350
New York, NY 10036-7901
www.siecus.org
The nation's best-known advocate for sex education.

Society for Adolescent Medicine
1916 NW Copper Oaks Circle
Blue Springs, MO 64015
www.adolescenthealth.org
The society may be able to help you find a physician in your area who specializes in health care for people ages 12–21.

VOICES in Action, Inc.
P.O. Box 148309
Chicago, Il. 60614
www.voices-action.org
A self-help group for survivors of incest, VOICES hosts a Web page for teens and links to other incest-help organizations.

HOTLINES YOU CAN CALL FOR HELP
(Copy and keep these numbers handy.
You never know when you might need one.)

ADVICE (on any matter)
Teen Help   1-800-840-5704

AIDS
AIDS Hotline   1-800- FOR-AIDS
CDC AIDS Information   1-800-342-2437
The Teen AIDS Hotline   1-800-440-TEEN

CHILD ABUSE
National Child Abuse Hotline   1-800-4-A-CHILD

CONTRACEPTION
Planned Parenthood   1-800-230-PLAN
Emergency Contraception Hotline   1-888-NOT2-LATE

CRISIS

| Crisis Helpline (for any kind of crisis) | 1-800 233-4357 |
| Youth Crisis Hotline | 1-800 448-4663 |

PREGNANCY

America's Crisis Pregnancy Helpline	1-800-67-BABY-6
Alcohol, Drug and Pregnancy	1-800-368-BABY
Teen Pregnancy Hotline	1-800-522-5006

RAPE, INCEST, SEXUAL ASSAULT

| Rape & Abuse & Incest National Network | 1-800-656-HOPE |

SEXUAL ORIENTATION

| National Gay and Lesbian Hotline | 1-888-843-4564 |

STDs

| National Sexually Transmitted Disease Hotline | 1-800-227-8922 |

VIOLENCE AT HOME

| National Domestic Violence Hotline | 1-800-799-7233 |

NOTES

Foreword

1. "Family, Money, Faith More Important Than Sex, Survey Reveals," *Jet* (May 17, 1999).
2. Debra W. Haffner, *Beyond the Big Talk: Every Parent's Guide to Raising Sexually Healthy Teens—From Middle School to High School and Beyond* (New York: Newmarket, 2001), p. 6.

A Note About AIDS

1. Gregory M. Herek, John P. Capitanio, and Keith F. Widaman, "HIV-Related Stigma and Knowledge in the United States: Prevalence and Trends, 1991–1999," *American Journal of Public Health* (March 1, 2002).
2. Quoted in "Ignorance of How HIV Is Spread Has Increased in US," Reuters Health Information, 2002.

Chapter 1

1. "Female Body Quiz: Facts and Myths Exposed," MayoClinic Healthy Living Centers at www.MayoClinic.com.
2. June M. Reinisch and Ruth Beasley, *The Kinsey Institute New Report on Sex: What You Must Know to Be Sexually Literate* (New York: St. Martin's Press, 1990), p. 278.

3. Thomas K. Hearn Jr., "In the 1960s There Was No Free Love—In the 1990s There Is No Safe Sex," *Journal of American College Health* (May 1994), p. 298.

4. As reported in Robert T. Brown, "Adolescent Sexuality at the Dawn of the 21st Century," *Adolescent Medicine: State of the Art Reviews* (February 2000), pp. 19–33. Primary sources cited as Harris and Associates, *Sexual Material on American Network Television During the 1987–88 Season* (New York: Planned Parenthood Federation of America, 1988); and *The Henry J. Kaiser Family Foundation Report: Sex on TV*, The Henry J. Kaiser Family Foundation (1999).

5. D. Kirby, *No Easy Answers: Research Findings on Programs to Reduce Teen Pregnancy* (Washington, D.C.: National Campaign to Prevent Teen Pregnancy), 1997.

6. Centers for Disease Control and Prevention. "Youth Risk Behavior Surveillance—United States, 1999," *Morbidity and Mortality Weekly Report CDC Surveillance Summaries* (June 9, 2000), pp. 1–96.

7. Centers for Disease Control and Prevention. "Youth Risk Behavior Surveillance—United States, 1993," *Morbidity and Mortality Weekly Report* (March 24, 1995), pp. 1–55.

8. Reinisch and Beasley, p. 13.

9. C. Ryan and D. Futterman, "Identity Development," in *Lesbian and Gay Youth: Care and Counseling. State of the Art Review of Adolescent Medicine*, vol. 8 (1997), p. 211.

10. Amy C. Butler, "Trends in Same-Gender Sexual Partnering, 1988–1998," *The Journal of Sex Research* (November 2000), pp. 333–343.

11. People for the American Way Foundation (Annual 1993–1999). *Hostile Climate: A State by State Report on Anti-Gay Activity* (Washington, D.C.: People for the American Way).

12. Letitia Anne Peplau and Linda D. Garnets, "A New Paradigm for Understanding Women's Sexuality and Sexual Orientation," *Journal of Social Issues* (Summer 2000), pp. 329–350.

13. Adapted from R.R. Troiden, "Homosexual Identity Development," *Journal of Adolescent Health* (1988), p. 112.

14. L.M. Diamond, "Sexual Identity, Attractions, and Behavior Among Young Sexual-Minority Women Over a Two-Year Period," *Developmental Psychology* (March 2000), pp. 241–250.

15. "Fact Sheet: Lesbian, Gay, Bisexual and Transgender Youth Issues," *SIECUS Report* (April/May 2001).

16. Margaret Blythe and Susan Rosenthal, "Female Adolescent Sexuality:

Promoting Healthy Sexual Development," *Obstetrics and Gynecology Clinics of North America* (March 2000), pp. 135–141.

17. American Psychological Association, "Answers to Your Questions About Sexual Orientation and Homosexuality," APA Public Information Web site at www.apa.org/pubinfo/answers.html

18. Quoted in Barry Yeoman, "Gay No More?" *Psychology Today* (April 1999), pp. 26–29+.

19. "APA Position Statements Pertinent to Gay and Lesbian Issues," December 1998, American Psychiatric Association, full statement available at www.psych.org.

20. Robert Spitzer, "200 Subjects Who Claim to Have Changed their Sexual Orientation from Homosexual to Heterosexual," Presentation at the American Psychiatric Association Annual Convention, New Orleans, May 9, 2001.

21. Rachel Rokicki, "Gay Debate," *Psychology Today* (September/October 2000), p. 11.

22. "Prominent Psychiatrist Announces New Study Results: Some Gays CAN Change," Press release from the National Association for Research and Therapy of Homosexuality, May 9, 2001.

23. Mackay, p. 24.

24. "Ambiguous Genitalia: When Gender Is Unclear at Birth," at www.MayoClinic.com, April 25, 2001.

25. Lisa Melton, "New Perspectives on the Management of Intersex," The Lancet (June 30, 2001), p. 2110.

26. "Ambiguous Genitalia," at www.MayoClinic.com

27. Mackay, p. 24.

28. "Hopkins Research Shows Nature, Not Nurture, Determines Gender," Office of Communication and Public Affairs, Johns Hopkins Medical Institutions, May 12, 2000. Report of a presentation at the Lawrence Wilkins Pediatric Endocrine Society meeting in Boston, that date.

29. Quoted in "Headline Watch: Gender and 'Sex Reassignment,'" May 16, 2000, at www.MayoClinic.com

30. Quoted in "Gender Determined in Womb," Associated Press, May 12, 2000.

31. J. Michael Bailey and Richard C. Pillard. " A Genetic Study of Male Sexual Orientation," *Archives of General Psychiatry* (1991), pp. 1089–96.

32. Bailey and Pillard.

33. Robert Pool, "Evidence for Homosexuality Gene," *Science* (July 16, 1993), pp. 291–92; Dean H. Hamer, Stella Hu, Victoria L. Magnuson, Nan Hu, and Angela M. L. Pattatucci, "A Linkage Between DNA Markers on the X

Chromosome and Male Sexual Orientation," *Science* (July 16, 1993), pp. 321–326.

34. S. Zhang and W.F. Odenwald, "Misexpression of the White (w) Gene Triggers Male-Male Courtship in Drosophila," *Proceedings of the National Academy of Sciences* (June 1995), pp. 5525–29.

35. George Rice, Carol Anderson, Neil Risch, and George Ebers, "Male Homosexuality: Absence of Linkage to Microsatellite Markers at Xq28," *Science* (April 23, 1999), pp. 665–67.

36. Kendler, Kenneth S., et al., "Sexual Orientation in a U.S. National Sample of Twin and Nontwin Sibling Pairs," *American Journal of Psychiatry* (November 2000, p. 1843).

37. Claudia Dreifus, "A Conversation with Anne Fausto-Sterling: Exploring What Makes Us Male or Female," *The New York Times* (January 2, 2001).

38. Quoted in Stanton Peele and Richard DeGrandpre, "My Genes Made Me Do It," *Psychology Today* (July 17, 1995), p. 50.

39. Lauren Neergaard (Associated Press), "Chromosome Study Counters Current Evidence of 'Gay Gene,'" *The Northern New Jersey Record* (April 23, 1999).

Chapter 2

1. Mackay, p. 16.

2. Christopher B. Cutter, "Compounded Percutaneous Testosterone Gel: Use and Effects in Hypogonadal Men," *Journal of the American Board of Family Practice* (2001), pp. 22–32.

3. "What Is Male Hypogonadism?" May 17, 2001 at www.MayoClinic.com.

4. June M. Reinisch and Ruth Beasley, *The Kinsey Institute New Report on Sex: What You Must Know to Be Sexually Literate* (New York: St. Martin's Press, 1990), p. 39.

5. Michael B. Brooks, "Epididymitis," *eMedicine Journal* (February 28, 2001) at www.emedicine.com.

6. Mark Zwanger and Timothy Rupp, "Testicular Torsion," *eMedicine Journal* (September 18, 2001) at www.emedicine.com.

7. Estimate from the American Society for Aesthetic Plastic Surgery, 2001.

8. "Engorged Breasts in Young Men," Men's Health Questions and Answers at www.camyclinic.com.

9. M.G. Haselton and D.M. Buss, "Error Management Theory: A New Perspective on Biases in Cross-Sex Mind Reading," *Journal of Personality and Social Psychology* (January 2000), pp. 81–91.

10. For more, see John Gerofi, "Latex Condom Manufacture," in *Condoms*, Adrian Mindel, ed. (London: BMJ Books, 2000), pp. 19–32.
11. W.P. Schellstede, M.P. Feinberg, and G. Dallabetta, "Condom Availability: Barriers to Access, Barriers to Use," in *Condoms*, Adrian Mindel, ed. (London: BMJ Books, 2000), p. 160.
12. Priscilla Alexander, *Prostitution: A Difficult Issue for Feminists* (San Francisco: Cleis Press, 1987), p. 188.
13. B.R. Edlin, K.L. Irwin, S. Faruque, et al., "Intersecting Epidemics—Crack Cocaine Use and HIV Infection among Inner City Young Adults," *New England Journal of Medicine* (November 24, 1994), pp. 1422–27.
14. Adele Weiner, "Understanding the Social Needs of Streetwalking Prostitutes," *Social Work* (January, 1996).
15. Brad Lemley, "Isn't She Lovely?" *Discover* (February 2000), pp. 42-49.
16. Emma Young, "Kind and Considerate," *New Scientist* (June 18, 2001).

Chapter 3

1. Michael D. Lemonick, "Teens Before Their Time," *Time* (October 30, 2000), p. 68.
2. P.B. Kaplowitz, S.E. Oberfield, and the Drug and Therapeutics and Executive Committees of the Lawson Wilkins Pediatric Endocrine Society, "Reexamination of the Age Limit for Defining When Puberty Is Precocious in Girls in the United States: Implications for Evaluation and Treatment," *Pediatrics* (1999), pp. 936–41.
3. M.E. Herman-Giddens, E.J. Stora, R.C. Wasserman, et al. "Secondary Sexual Characteristics and Menses in Young Girls Seen in Office Practice: A Study from the Pediatric Research in Office Settings Network," *Pediatrics* (1997), pp. 505–12.
4. Herman-Giddens, Stora, Wasserman, et al.
5. A.M.K. Rickwood, S.E. Kenny, and S.C. Donnell, "Toward Evidence Based Circumcision of English Boys: Survey of Trends in Practice," *British Medical Journal* (September 30, 2000), pp. 792–93.
6. David L. Gollaher, *Circumcision: A History of the World's Most Controversial Surgery*, New York: Basic Books, 2000.
7. Mackay, p. 77.
8. Rickwood, Kenny, and Donnell, pp. 792–93.
9. Barbara Keesling, "Beyond Orgasmatron," *Psychology Today* (November 1999).

10. E.O. Laumann, J.H. Gagnon, R.T. Michael, and S. Michaels, *The Social Organization of Sexuality: Sexual Practices in the United States* (Chicago: University of Chicago Press, 1994), p. 114.

11. J. Bancroft, C.A. Graham, and C. McCord, "Conceptualizing Women's Sex Problems," *Journal of Sex and Marital Therapy* (2001), pp. 93–103.

12. Mark D. Levie, "Female Sexual Dysfunction: The Challenges of Treatment," Part I. Conference Report: Update in Gynecology from the American College of Obstetricians and Gynecologists Annual Clinical Meeting, April 28–May 2, 2001. *Medscape Women's Health* 6(3), 2001.

13. Josie Butcher, "ABCs of Sexual Health: Female Sexual Problems II: Sexual Pain and Sexual Fears," *British Medical Journal* (January 9, 1999).

14. Quoted in "Women Behaving Badly?" original article, WebMD at http://my.webmd.com/content/article/1689.51534.

15. "Women Behaving Badly?"

16. www.e-breasts.net

17. Zosia Kmietowica, "Health Department Misled Women over Breast Implants Risks, Groups Claim," *British Medical Journal* (March 31, 2001), pp. 322, 756.

18. Diane Zuckerman and Rachel Flynn, "Important Facts about Breast Implants," at http://www.cpr4womenandfamilies.org/implantfacts.html.

19. "The G-Spot: A Medical Myth," Reuters Medical News, August 28, 2001.

20. Claudia Holzman, Judith M. Leventhal, Hong Qiu, Nicole M. Jones, and Jenny Wang, "Factors Linked to Bacterial Vaginosis in Nonpregnant Women," *American Journal of Public Health* (October 2001), pp. 1664–70.

21. W. Steven Pray, "Treatment of Vaginal Fungal Infections," *U.S. Pharmacist* (2001).

22. Centers for Disease Control and Prevention, "1998 Guidelines for Treatment of Sexually Transmitted Diseases," *Morbidity and Mortality Weekly Report*, (1998), p. 75.

23. Pray.

24. American Society of Clinical Pathologists, "Cervical Cancer Facts," (2001).

25. P. Kestelman and J. Trussell, "Efficacy of the Simultaneous Use of Condoms and Spermicides," *Family Planning Perspectives* (1991), pp. 226–27+.

26. Quoted in Neil Osterweil, "What's Sex Got to Do with It? 'Normal' Sexual Function in Women Is a Matter of Opinion, Experts Say," *WebMD Medical News* (November 1, 2000).

27. Jeanne Davis, "Sex in the City: Women's Sex Lives, Up Close and Very Personal," *WebMD Medical News* (March 30, 2001).

28. Estimate reported by Family Health International.
29. World Health Organization estimate reported in "UK Doctors Given New Guidelines on Female Circumcision," *Reuters Medical News* (August 20, 2001).
30. Mackay, pp. 74–75.
31. I. Ebberfeld, "Anrüchig und Anziehend Zugleich," *Sexualmedizin* (1996), pp. 205–208. I. Ebberfeld, " Fetischismus Oder Ganz Normale Leidenschaft," *Sexualmedizin* (1997), pp. 234–242.
32. Helen Fisher, *Anatomy of Love: A Natural History of Mating, Marriage, and Why We Stray* (New York: Fawcett Columbine, 1992), p. 44.
33. S. Jacob, M. McClintock, B. Zelano, and C. Ober. "Paternally Inherited HLA Alleles Are Associated with Women's Choice of Male Odor," *Nature Genetics* (February 2002), pp. 175–179.
34. C. Wedekind, T. Seebeck, F. Bettens, and A.J. Paepke, "MHC-dependent Mate Preferences in Humans," *Proceedings of the Royal Society of London* (1995), pp. 245–249.

Chapter 4

1. L.A. Peplau and L.D. Garnets, "A New Paradigm for Understanding Women's Sexuality and Sexual Orientation," *Journal of Social Issues* (Summer 2000).
2. J.D. Baldwin and J.I. Baldwin, "Gender Differences in Sexual Interest," *Archives of Sexual Behavior* (1997), pp. 181–210.
3. B.C. Leigh, "Reasons for Having and Avoiding Sex: Gender, Sexual Orientation, and Relationship to Sexual Behavior," *Journal of Sex Research* (1989), pp. 199–209.
4. E. Hatfield, S. Sprecher, J.T. Pillemer, D. Greenberger, and P. Wexler. "Gender Differences in What Is Desired in the Sexual Relationship," *Journal of Psychology and Human Sexuality* (1989), pp. 39–52.
5. B. J. Ellis and D. Symons, "Sex Differences in Sexual Fantasy," *Journal of Sex Research* (1990), pp. 490–521.
6. Kaiser Family Foundation "National Survey of Teens: Teens Talk About Dating, Intimacy, and their Sexual Experiences," (Menlo Park, CA: The Foundation and *YM Magazine*, 1998).
7. R.T. Michael, J.H. Gagnon, E.O. Laumann, and Gina Kolata, *Sex in America: A Definitive Survey* (New York: Warner Books, 1995), p. 156.
8. June M. Reinisch and Ruth Beasley, *The Kinsey Institute New Report on Sex: What You Must Know to Be Sexually Literate* (New York: St. Martin's Press, 1990), p. 92.

9. G. Cowley, "The Biology of Beauty," *Newsweek* (June 3, 1996), pp. 60–65.

10. D. Singh, "Body Shape and Women's Attractiveness: The Critical Role of the Waist-to-Hip Ratio," *Human Nature* (1993), pp. 297–321.

11. A. Furnham, M. Lavancy, and A. McClelland. "Waist-to-Hip Ratio and Facial Attractiveness: A Pilot Study." *Personality and Individual Differences* (2001), pp. 491–502.

12. Wardell B. Pomeroy, *Boys and Sex* (New York: Delacorte, 1981), p. 15.

13. Data from www.scarleteen.com.

14. Pomeroy, p. 99.

15. Kaiser Family Foundation and *Seventeen* magazine, "SexSmarts: Decision Making," (Menlo Park, CA: The Foundation, 2000).

16. Centers for Disease Control and Prevention, "Youth Risk Behavior Surveillance—United States, 1999," *Morbidity and Mortality Weekly* (June 9, 2000), pp. 1–96.

17. R. Heffernan, M.A. Chiasson, and J. E. Sackoff. "HIV Risk Behaviors among Adolescents at a Sexually Transmitted Disease Clinic in New York City." *Journal of Adolescent Health* (1996), pp. 429–34.

18. "Youth Risk Behavior Surveillance—United States, 1999."

19. The Alan Guttmacher Institute, *Sex and America's Teenagers* (New York: AGI, 1994).

20. K.A. Moore and A. Driscoll, *Partners, Predators, Peers, Protectors: Males and Teen Pregnancy: New Data Analyses of the 1995 National Survey of Family Growth*, (Washington, D.C.: National Campaign to Prevent Teen Pregnancy, 1997).

21. *Sex and America's Teenagers.*

22. *Sex and America's Teenagers.*

23. J.D. Fortenberry, D.P. Orr, G.D. Zimet, and M.J. Blythe. "Weekly and Seasonal Variation in Sexual Behaviors among Adolescent Women with Sexually Transmitted Diseases," *Journal of Adolescent Health* (1997), pp. 420–25.

24. M.A. Schuster, R.M. Bell, and D.E. Kanouse. "The Sexual Practices of Adolescent Virgins: Genital Sexual Activities of High School Students Who Have Never Had Vaginal Intercourse," *American Journal of Public Health* (1997), pp. 1570–76.

25. B.C. Leigh, D M. Morrison, K. Trocki, and M.T. Temple, "Sexual Behavior of American Adolescents: Results from a U.S. National Survey." *Journal of Adolescent Health* (1994), pp. 117–25.

26. Andreas Bartels and Semir Zeki, "The Neural Basis of Romantic Love," *NeuroReport* (2000), pp. 3829–34.

27. Quoted in Barrie Gillies, "The Love Buzz: Why You Get High," *Cosmopolitan* (January 1998), p. 142.

28. National Campaign to Prevent Teen Pregnancy, *Not Just Another Thing to Do: Teens Talk about Sex, Regret, and the Influence of Their Parents* (Washington, D.C.: National Campaign to Prevent Teen Pregnancy, 2000).

29. Quoted in Angela Pirisi, "Sex: Once Is Enough," *Psychology Today* (September/October 2000), p. 16.

30. Laura Kann, Steven Kinchen, Barbara Williams, James Ross, Richard Lowry, Jo Anne Grunbaum, Lloyd Kolbe. "Youth Risk Behavior Surveillance—United States, 1999," CDC: *Morbidity and Mortality Weekly Report* (June 20, 2000), pp. 1–96.

31. Data from the National Campaign to Prevent Teen Pregnancy, 2001.

32. S. K. Henshaw. "Unintended Pregnancy in the United States," *Family Planning Perspectives* (1998), pp. 24–29+. Table 1.

33. Alan Guttmacher Institute, *Teenage Pregnancy: Overall Trends and State by State Information* (New York: AGI, 1999).

34. S.C. Curtin and J.A. Martin. "Births: Preliminary Data for 1999." *National Vital Statistics Reports* (2000), p. 14.

35. S. Singh and J.E. Darroch. "Adolescent Pregnancy and Childbearing: Levels and Trends in Developed Countries," *Family Planning Perspectives* (2000), pp. 14-23.

36. Data from the National Center for Health Statistics, 1995.

37. C. S. Haignere, R. Gold, and H.J. McDaniel, "Adolescent Abstinence and Condom Use: Are We Sure We Are Really Teaching What Is Safe?" *Health Education & Behavior* (February 1999), pp. 43–54.

38. National Campaign to Prevent Teen Pregnancy, *Risky Business: A 2000 Poll. Teens Tell Us What They Really Think of Contraception and Sex* (Washington, D.C.: National Campaign to Prevent Teen Pregnancy: 2000).

39. Center for Reproductive Law and Policy, "Parental Consent and Notice for Contraceptives Threatens Teen Health and Constitutional Rights," April, 2001, available at www.crlp.org.

40. Elizabeth L. Paul, "'Hookups: Characteristics and Correlated of College Students' Spontaneous and Anonymous Sexual Experiences," *Journal of Sex Research* (February 2000).

41. Edward O. Laumann, Anthony Paik, and Raymond C. Rosen, "Sexual Dysfunction in the United States Prevalence and Predictors," *Journal of the American Medical Association* (February 10, 1999), pp. 537–44.

42. F.A. DiBlasio and B.B. Benda. "Adolescent Sexual Behavior: Multivariate Analysis of a Social Learning Model," *Journal of Adolescent Research* (1994), pp. 449–66.

43. CDC Youth Surveillance Data, 1999.

44. S.G. Millstein, A.B. Moscicki, and J.M. Broering. "Female Adolescents at High, Moderate, and Low Risk of Exposure to HIV: Differences in Knowledge, Beliefs, and Behavior," *Journal of Adolescent Health* (1993), pp. 133–42.

45. K.L. Graves and B.C. Leigh, "The Relationship of Substance Use to Sexual Activity among Young Adults in the United States." *Family Planning Perspectives* (1995), pp. 18–22+.

46. J. Jaccard, P.J. Dittus, and W. Gordon, "Maternal Correlates of Adolescent Sexual and Contraceptive Behavior," *Family Planning Perspectives* (1996), pp. 156–65+.

47. D. Holtzman and R. Rubinson, "Parent and Peer Communication Effects on AIDS-Related Behavior among U.S. High School Students," *Family Planning Perspectives* (1995), pp. 235–40+.

48. Kaiser Family Foundation "National Survey of Teens: Teens Talk About Dating, Intimacy, and Their Sexual Experiences," Menlo Park, CA: The Foundation and *YM Magazine*, 1998.

49. Daniel Wight, Marion Henderson, Gillian Raab, Charles Abraham, Katie Buston, and Graham Hart, "Extent of Regretted Sexual Intercourse among Young Teenagers in Scotland: A Cross-Sectional Survey," *British Medical Journal* (May 6, 2000), pp. 1243–44.

50. K.A. Moore et al., *A Statistical Portrait of Adolescent Sex, Contraception and Childbearing. March 1998.* The National Campaign to Prevent Teen Pregnancy (Washington D.C.: Data based on the 1995 National Survey of Family Growth).

Chapter 5

1. Personal communication and book excerpt from Deborah M. Roffman, *Sex and Sensibility: The Thinking Parent's Guide to Talking Sense about Sex* (New York: Perseus, 2000).

2. "How Things Work—Young and Old," Mayo Clinic Healthy Living Centers, Osborne's complete interview at www.MayoClinic.com/home?id=HQ01363.

3. American Medical Association, *Diagnostic and Treatment Guidelines on Child Sexual Abuse* (Chicago: American Medical Association, 1992).

4. Anita Raj, "Is Sexual Abuse Related to Increased Sexual Risk Taking among Male and Female High School Students?" *1999 National HIV Prevention Conference* presentation.

5. J. Coid, A. Petruckevitch, G. Feder, Wai-Shan Chung, J. Richardson, and S. Moorey, "Relation between Childhood Sexual and Physical Abuse and Risk of Revictimisation in Women: A Cross-Sectional Survey," *The Lancet* (August 11, 2001), pp. 358: 450.

6. Personal communication.

7. Diann M. Ackard and Dianne Neumark-Sztainer, "Date Violence and Date Rape among Adolescents: Associations with Disordered Eating Behaviors and Psychological Health," Presented at the 109th Annual Convention of the American Psychological Association, San Francisco, CA, August 2001. Published in *Child Abuse and Neglect* (2002).

8. P. Tjaden and N. Thoennes, "Full Report of the Prevalence, Incidence, and Consequences of Violence Against Women: Findings from the National Violence Against Women Survey," U.S. Department of Justice: November 2000, p. iv.

9. Callie Marie Rennison, "Criminal Victimization 2000: Changes 1999–2000 with Trends 1993–2000," (June 2001) U.S. Department of Justice Programs, U.S. Department of Justice, NCJ 187007.

10. Calculation from RAINN (Rape, Abuse and Incest National Network) based on 2000 National Crime Victimization Survey. U.S. Department of Justice.

11. Tjaden and Thoennes.

12. Patrick A. Langan and Caroline W. Harlow, "Child Rape Victims, 1992), June 1994 Crime Data Brief, U.S. Department of Justice, Bureau of Justice Statistics, Publication number NCJ-147001.

13. Langan and Harlow.

14. Rennison.

15. Rennison.

16. D. Finkelhor, "Current Information on the Scope and Nature of Child Sexual Abuse," *Child Abuse and Neglect* (1994), pp. 31–53.

17. Rennison.

18. Tjaden and Thoennes.

19. Lauren E. Duncan, "Gender Role Socialization and Male-on-Male vs. Female-on-Male Child Sexual Abuse," *Sex Roles: A Journal of Research* (November 1998).

20. William C. Holmes and Gail B. Slap, "Sexual Abuse of Boys: Definition,

Prevalence, Correlates, Sequelae, and Management," *Journal of the American Medical Association*, (December 2, 1998), pp. 1855–62.

21. Jessica Vitkus and M. Ingall, *Smart Sex* (New York: Pocket Books, 1998), p. 272.

22. Holmes and Slap.

23. K.L. Graves and B.C. Leigh. "The Relationship of Substance Use to Sexual Activity among Young Adults in the United States," *Family Planning Perspectives* (1995), pp. 18–22+.

24. "Risk Taking Strongly Influenced by Sense of Control, Says UGA Researcher," University of Georgia Public Affairs News Bureau (November 20, 2001).

25. American Social Health Association/Kaiser Family Foundation, *STDs in America* (1998).

26. Henry J. Kaiser Family Foundation and *YM Magazine*, "National Survey of Teens: Teens Talk about Dating, Intimacy, and their Sexual Experiences." (Menlo Park, CA: The Foundation, 1998).

27. Adrian Mindel, ed., *Condoms* (London: BMJ Books, 2000), p. ix.

28. Data from National Center for HIV, STD and TB Prevention, Divisions of HIV/AIDS Prevention, August 20, 2001, at www.cdc.gov.

29. Kenneth H. Fife, Commentary (on HPV Treatments), Sexually Transmitted Disease Information Center, *The Journal of the American Medical Association* at www.ama-assn.org.

30. L. Koutsky, "Epidemiology of Genital Human Papillomavirus Infection," *American Journal of Medicine* (May 1997), pp. 3–8.

31. Erika C. Lambert, "College Students' Knowledge of Human Papillomavirus and Effectiveness of a Brief Educational Intervention," *Journal of the American Board of Family Practitioners* (2001), pp. 178–83.

32. Fife.

33. Centers for Disease Control and Prevention, 1998 Guidelines for Treatment of Sexually Transmitted Diseases. *Morbidity and Mortality Weekly Report* (1998), p. 88

34. Mark D. Levie, "Human Papillomavirus and Cervical Disease; Part 2. Update in Gynecology from the American College of Obstetricians and Gynecologists Annual Clinical Meeting, 2001," April 28–May 2, 2001, *Medscape Women's Health* (2001).

35. K. M. Stone, "Human Papillomavirus Infection and Genital Warts: Update on Epidemiology and Treatment, *Clinical Infectious Diseases* 1995: 20 (Supplement 1): S91–S97.

36. Levie.

37. "Task Force Calls for Chlamydia, Lipid Screening," press release from the Agency for Healthcare Research and Quality (AHRQ), April 18, 2001.

38. "Task Force Calls for Chlamydia, Lipid Screening."

39. "Task Force Calls for Chlamydia, Lipid Screening."

40. "U.S. Syphilis Rate Hit All-Time Low in 2000," Reuters Medical News, November 28, 2001.

41. Centers for Disease Control and Prevention, 1998 Guidelines for Treatment of Sexually Transmitted Diseases. *Morbidity and Mortality Weekly Report* (1998), p. 59.

42. K.K. Fox, W.L. Whittington, W.C. Levine. J.S. Moran, A.A. Zaidi, and A.K. Nakashima. "Gonorrhea in the United States, 1981–1996. Demographic and Geographic Trends," *Sexually Transmitted Diseases* (1998), pp. 386–393.

43. Susan Drake, Stephen Taylor, David Brown, and Deenan Pillay, "Improving the Care of Patients with Genital Herpes," *British Medical Journal* (September 9, 2000), pp. 619–23.

44. Centers for Disease Control and Prevention, 1998 Guidelines for Treatment of Sexually Transmitted Diseases. *Morbidity and Mortality Weekly Report* (1998), p. 20.

45. Tao G. Kassler and D.B. Rein, "Medical Care Expenditures for Genital Herpes in the United States," *Sexually Transmitted Diseases* (2000), pp. 32–38.

46. J. D. Fortenberry, E. J. Brizendine, B.P. Katz, K.K. Woods, M.J. Blythe, and D.P. Orr. "Subsequent Sexually Transmitted Infections among Adolescent Women with Genital Infection Due to Chlamydia trachomatis, Neisseria gonorrhoeae, or Trichomonas vaginalis." *Sexually Transmitted Diseases* (1999), pp. 26–32.

47. Anna Wald and Katherine Link, "Risk of Human Immunodeficiency Virus Infection in Herpes Simplex Type-2 Seropositive Persons: A Meta-analysis," *The Journal of Infectious Diseases* (January 1, 2002).

48. F. Sorvillo, L. Smith, P. Kerndt, and L. Ash, "Trichomonas vaginalis, HIV, and African-Americans," *Emerging Infectious Diseases* (Centers for Disease Control, November-December 2001).

49. The Henry J. Kaiser Family Foundation and *Seventeen*, "SexSmarts: Decision Making: A Series of National Surveys of Teens about Sex," September 2000. KFF Publication #3148.

50. Charlotte Davis Kasl, *Women, Sex, and Addiction: A Search for Love and Power* (New York, Ticknor, 1989). Quote from page 27.

51. "Compulsive Sexual Behavior," Healthy Living Centers: Relationships at www.MayoClinic.com.

52. CDC "Youth Risk Behavior Surveillance" reports, 1993, 1995, 1997, 1999. Various Authors. All published in *Morbidity and Mortality Weekly Report*.

53. National Campaign to Prevent Teen Pregnancy, *Not Just Another Thing to Do: Teens Talk about Sex, Regret, and the Influence of Their Parents* (Washington, D.C.: National Campaign to Prevent Teen Pregnancy, 2000).

54. Kaiser Family Foundation and *YM* magazine.

55. "Trends in Sexual Risk Behaviors among High School Students—United States, 1991-1997." *Morbidity and Mortality Weekly* (September 18, 1998), pp. 749–752.

56. *Not Just Another Thing to Do: Teens Talk about Sex, Regret, and the Influence of Their Parents.*

In Closing

1. Victor S. Johnston, *Why We Feel: The Science of Human Emotions* (Reading, MA: Perseus Books, 1999). Original poem published with permission of its author.

INDEX

Page numbers in *italics* refer to illustrations.